Finding Freedom

Finding Freedom is based on
two previous books by Joyce Huggett:

Growing into Freedom
Living Free

Finding Freedom:

Becoming the Person
God Made Me to Be

Joyce Huggett

Hodder & Stoughton

LONDON SYDNEY AUCKLAND

Copyright © Joyce Huggett 1994

Cover: author photograph courtesy of
The Scripture Union

First published in Great Britain in 1994
by Hodder and Stoughton Ltd,
a division of Hodder Headline PLC

The right of Joyce Huggett to be identified as the author
of this work has been asserted by her in accordance with the
Copyright, Designs and Patents Act 1988.

10 9 8 7 6 5 4 3 2 1

British Library Cataloguing in Publication Data

CIP catalogue record for this title is
available from the British Library

ISBN 0 340 59986 3

Typeset by Hewer Text Composition Services, Edinburgh
Printed and bound in Great Britain by
Cox & Wyman, Reading, Berks.

Hodder and Stoughton Ltd
A Division of Hodder Headline PLC
338 Euston Road
London NW1 3BH

For Pauline
with love and thanks

Bible references which are not taken from the NIV are quoted with the following abbreviations:

AV   Authorised Version
GNB   Good News Bible © 1976
JB   Jerusalem Bible © 1966
JBP   J. B. Phillips
KJV   King James Version
LB   The Living Bible © 1974

ACKNOWLEDGMENTS

Whenever I finish a book, I find myself overwhelmed by the number of people who partner me in the writing. This book has been no exception but, as always, there is room here to mention only a few.

First, I would like to thank Carolyn Armitage, Editorial Director at Hodder and Stoughton for suggesting that *Living Free* was worth revising. But for her encouragement, I would not have embarked on this project.

Next, I am indebted to my friend and editor James Catford for all the affirmation he has given me both in the past when we have worked together on other books and, in particular, for the way he has believed in the contents of *Living Free* and this revision of that book. Having the opportunity to be back in touch with him and (through him) his wife Clare has been a very great joy.

Then, as always, I want to thank my husband who has given me even more support than usual while I have been giving birth to this 'baby'. He has read each chapter, given me shrewd and thought-provoking critiques and done much of the cooking to release me to write. For these gifts, I am humbled and grateful.

My computer 'died' while I was writing Chapter Ten. So many people rallied round me during the crisis that I felt very cared for. In particular, I would like to thank Derek Knell and Andy Russell of FEBA Radio, David and Margaret Judson of MECO and Carl Armerding at Schloss Mittersill for their help and concern.

Finally, I owe a debt of gratitude to two other groups of people: those who have given me permission to tell their stories to illustrate this book and those who have prayed for the book's conception. Where I have drawn on the experience and testimonies of friends and acquaintances, I have changed their names to protect their privacy but I want the people behind the pseudonyms to know that I am grateful to them for allowing their stories to be used to help others. I am awed, too, that so many of our prayer supporters committed themselves to pray for the book's gestation and growth and for me as I gave birth to it. Their ministry means more to me than I can say. To them and the many readers who have spurred me on by writing to ask when the book is to be published, I also express my appreciation in that simple but profound word, THANKYOU.

My appreciation for permission to quote extracts from various books are due to the following publishers:

Ave Maria Press, Inc., Notre Dame, IN 46556, for: *With Open Hands* by Henri Nouwen (© 1972) pp. 24–5; *Healing* by Francis MacNutt (© 1974) pp 100–1, 116–17; *Heal My Heart, O Lord* by Joan Hutson (© 1976) pp. 104–5; *Praying Our Goodbyes* by Joyce Rupp OSM (© 1988) p. 128. All rights reserved.
Paulist Press for *Hope for the Flowers* by Torina Paulus (© 1972) pp. 21–3; *The Way of Tenderness* by Kevin O Shea CSSR (© 1978 by The Missionary Society of St Paul the Apostle in the State of New York) pp. 111–13, 118.

CONTENTS

AUTHOR'S PREFACE

An author's burden frequently gives birth to a book. That, at least, has been my experience. I have carried the burden from which this book emerged for the past twelve years or so, though, during that time, the nature of the burden has gradually changed and evolved.

Let me explain. Twelve years ago, my husband and I were frequently invited to speak at conferences for Christian students. At this time, we were often deeply moved by the zeal, the dedication and the commitment to Christ which was being expressed by some of the fine young people we met. But one thing concerned us. Whereas each student was clearly full of personal, God-given potential, many of them seemed afraid of giving expression to the person God had created them to be and seemed, instead, to be struggling to model themselves on some of the Christian heroes of the day – like John Stott, for example. 'They even try to speak like him,' I observed to my husband on one occasion after I had heard a student attempt to give a scholarly book review.

'Why don't you write a book to help such people?' my then editor invited. I did. As I wrote it, I toyed with the idea of calling it *No Cardboard Cut-outs* because one of my aims was to show that God did not create us to become a replica of anyone else. As someone has expressed it, 'When God made you, he broke the mould.' Since that title sounded rather negative, I chose, instead, to call the book *Growing Into Freedom*, a title which later became *Living Free* and now *Finding Freedom*.

This year sees the tenth anniversary of the publication of the original book.

I now no longer move in student circles, live in Cyprus and work for the church overseas. This work takes me to some fascinating parts of the world and I have found that, on my travels, that old burden keeps bothering me. Now, it is not students that concern me but older, often more experienced Christians. They concern me because, although they may be older in years and older in the faith in many cases, the trend seems to be the same. Many of them still strive to become like their heroes in the faith – like Graham Kendrick or John Wimber. And the 'dis-ease' has spread so that it is no longer only individuals who are caught in this trap. Whole fellowships seem collectively to have been ensnared so that while individual Christians are striving to become miniature versions of the platform speakers they most admire, church fellowships try to ape the latest John Wimber meeting or the most recent round of Spring Harvest gatherings.

I am not knocking John Wimber, Graham Kendrick or Spring Harvest. All of these have produced much fruit for the Kingdom and in this I rejoice. What concerns me still is that many Christians have not discerned that God only made one John Wimber and one Graham Kendrick; that this same God created each of us to play faithfully our note without which the great symphony of life will be incomplete.

It seemed important, therefore, to celebrate the tenth year of this book's life by up-dating it, expanding it and publishing this completely revised new edition under a different title and with a different dust jacket. The kernel of the book is the same. And the burden is the same. I long that every Christian person should enter into the freedom which is our heritage as people who are children of God. But, inevitably, over the past years, my perception has changed as I have changed to become, I trust, far more like the person God always created me to be. The thrust of the book is therefore somewhat different. I trust that the original kernel and the new material in which this is now embedded will encourage today's Christian people to find answers to that question which nags at many of us from time to time: 'How can I become the person God always created me to be?' If the revised version of *Living Free* achieves that aim, it will be an anniversary worth celebrating.

1

INSTANT FREEDOM

Someone called Sue once gave me a banner she had made. On a background of blue felt, she had stitched a large, black cross at the foot of which stood two figures. Their backs were turned on a pile of broken chains, their faces were tilted as they contemplated the cross and their arms were raised in ecstasy. Two yellow words soared over the jubilant scene: 'Free indeed'.

I hung the banner in the place where I used to retreat to pray. Sometimes, as I gazed at it, my mind would wander to Ron, a member of the church where I worshipped. A few weeks earlier, Ron's eyes had met mine in the middle of a sermon. The preacher was making some startling claims:

'Jesus heals broken bodies and brings people out of darkness into light. It is possible to rub shoulders with Jesus and yet remain the same person. It is also possible to touch Jesus and be radically changed. We read of the woman with a haemorrhage in Luke 8. She reached out and touched him and "immediately her bleeding stopped". The power of Jesus flowed into her life and she was made whole – completely new. Free.'

A few weeks earlier, Ron had confided in me that he waged a constant war against the lust and sexual fantasies which seemed to hold him in a vice-like grip. He had confessed that this battle left him weary and defeated. Although he frequently stretched out his hand, as it were, and touched the hem of Jesus's garment, no release had come. He had prayed and prayed to be radically changed to become the person God created him to be, but nothing seemed to alter. In the middle of the sermon, his eyes asked a question: 'If Jesus could change that woman instantly, why hasn't he done the same for me? What's wrong with me? Why was hers such a big success story while mine has "failure" written across it?'

When I gazed at the banner hanging there in my prayer room, my heart would go out to Ron and I would ask myself a question: 'Why were the two yellow felt figures so jubilant while Ron remains so defeated?' Then I would think of my own spiritual pilgrimage and of the Christians I meet in the course of my travels and I would ask: 'Why do we Christians so frequently fail in our struggle to become the people our Creator made us to be, and why do we feel frustrated when God loves us so much that, in Christ, he died to secure our freedom?'

Over a period of time, as I prayed the question, an answer evolved. There is a sense in which sermons like the one I have quoted raise false expectations in people like Ron. The Bible nowhere suggests that total, immediate freedom and Christian maturity are experiences enjoyed in all their fullness this side of eternity. The Bible writers envisage Christians enjoying a freedom which comes in instalments and a maturity which develops only gradually and a total transformation which only reaches completion the other side of eternity.

There is another sense, on the other hand, in which the preacher was quite correct to suggest that, when we hand over the reins of our lives to Christ, we can be radically changed because freedom's first instalment comes in the form of salvation. By salvation I mean deliverance from guilt and from the past, deliverance from sin's penalty and from its enslavement, freedom to call God 'Father' and to enjoy intimacy with him, to name but a few of the faces of this multi-faceted gift. As Paul puts it, in Jesus 'we gain our freedom, the forgiveness of our sins' (Colossians 1:13, JB).

The cost of freedom

Christians who can pin-point a time and place in their life when, by faith, they surrendered to the love of God often seem intoxicated by joy for a while. Like the figures in my banner, they feel gloriously different, exhilaratingly free and seem quite uninhibited in giving expression to their joy.

A friend of mine has recently taken the first few intoxicating sips of this joy. She is a tonic to be with. Her eyes sparkle. Her face shines. She is the same as she always was, yet strangely different. Her attitudes are more Christ-like than they used to be. She seems unable to stop marvelling at God's gift of salvation. She is gloriously free. A new creation in very many ways – much more like the person I imagine God created her to be. But she would be the first to admit that she is not yet mature in Christ. Far from it. Whole layers of her personality have yet to be enlightened so that they respond to God.

Christians who have never been encountered by God with a dramatic, Damascus-road-type conversion, on the other hand, are often painfully aware that maturing in Christ takes a life-time. They know, deep down in their innermost beings, that God has set them free but this assurance does not necessarily excite them. Some take their freedom for granted. Others have lost sight of it. For many it has become a mundane part of life like cleaning their teeth or catching the commuter train. God's good news can leave them cold and unmoved, either because it has lodged in their heads and never trickled into their hearts or because they have become so over-familiar with the implications of it that they have lost the ability to marvel at the mystery of it all.

Often, when I detect this kind of indifference lurking in the crevices of my own heart, I reflect on a story Archbishop Anthony Bloom tells. The story is of Natalie, a Russian woman of whom little is known except her name and the fact that she lived in Russia at the turn of the century, when civil war ravaged her country.

As war swept through that land, city after city fell prey to one army after another. In a town which had fallen into the hands of the Red Army, the wife of an officer in the White Army seemed to be caught in a human web. If enemy soldiers discovered her, she and her two children would be killed instantly. What could she do to preserve their lives?

On the outskirts of the city, she discovered a small, wooden cabin. She could hide there until the first surges of conflict were over. Then she would escape.

Towards evening on her second day in hiding, she heard someone knocking on the cabin door. Full of fear, she opened it to discover a young woman of her own age. It was Natalie. She spoke in urgent whispers. 'You must flee at once. You've been discovered. Tonight the soldiers will come. You are to be shot.'

The mother looked down at her two small children. Escape? How could she escape? Her children were too young to walk far. They would be recognised at once. The plan was unthinkable. She must prepare to die.

But Natalie persisted.

'Don't worry about the children. I'll stay here. They won't even look for you.'

'You stay here? But they'll kill you.'

'Yes. But I have no children.'

That night Natalie returned. The mother and her two small boys escaped into the woods. Natalie faced the soldiers alone. Natalie faced death – another woman's death – alone. At any moment, she could have stepped out of the wooden cabin. At any moment she could have become Natalie again. At any moment she could have stepped into freedom. She chose not to. She chose, instead, to stay inside the cabin.

Hours passed. With the cold of morning they came. Members of the Red Army battered down the door and, without bothering to drag her outside, shot her where she was – in bed. That is where friends found her later that day. Dead.

The reason why I like to meditate on that example of self-sacrifice is that it reminds me that two thousand years earlier, a young man of Natalie's age awaited his own death. He was the God-man, Jesus. Just as Natalie died in place of the young mother, so Jesus died in my place. Just as the price Natalie paid was her life-blood, so the price Jesus paid to secure my freedom was his shed blood. I find this awesome and humbling. And I find it even more awesome that God was in Christ giving us a fresh start by forgiving our sins (2 Corinthians 5:19).

This surely must mean that, when the Son suffered the agony

of the Crucifixion, the Father suffered with him. I sometimes seem to see, with the eyes of my imagination, the Father, like a giant shadow, standing behind his Son as he hangs on the Cross. As the nails are hammered into the hands of Jesus, they penetrate the Father's hands also. As the spear pierces Jesus's side, it pierces the Father's also.[1] And I reflect that the Father and the Son suffered, among other things, that I might be set free to become the person God created me to be.

Freedom from guilt

This is deep mystery. Trying to translate a mystery into words is rather like trying to describe a sunset to a person born blind or an oratorio to a person born deaf. It cannot be adequately done. A mystery yields its secrets gradually and slowly to those who pause to ponder, to meditate and to reflect.

I was reminded of this while I was leading a retreat on one occasion. One of the retreatants confessed to feeling a certain distance separating her from God. The reason, she knew, was not that she had committed any spectacular sin which might hit the headlines of the Christian press, yet she discerned a sense of unworthiness as she attempted to spend quality time with God. This seemed to be hindering her spiritual and emotional growth. So I suggested to her that she might spend some time meditating, that is, chewing over and responding to, the meaning of Christ's death. She did. Next day, a hush seemed to descend on the woodland glade where we sat as, with awe and wonder, I examined the pictures she had drawn as a result of her meditation.

The sketch depicted herself with Jesus. From her flowed a polluted stream which flowed into the Saviour. From him flowed a red river of forgiving love which flowed into her and circulated all around her body injecting her with new life. 'It's like a blood transfusion,' she said with a smile. 'All the anti-bodies which were eating me up have gone. They've been replaced by life-giving blood.'

As I studied the pictures and listened to her story, my own love for God was rekindled as I recalled afresh that he loves us so much that, when we come to him, he flushes from us the sin and guilt which soil our lives and renews us with his own life – even when we *have* committed crimes for which we would now condemn ourselves. Like the elderly woman who once told me her story:

> I've lived a terrible life. At times I've been quite evil and done really terrible things. Now I'm growing old, I thought to myself: 'I'd love to go and live near my two beautiful grandchildren.' But my daughter knows the kind of life I've led. Maybe she wouldn't want her mother so near? After all, I could influence her children, couldn't I?
>
> One day I told my daughter what was going on in my mind. She's a Christian and do you know what she said? 'Why don't you put your trust in Jesus, Mummy? He can wipe out the past, set you free from it, give you a completely new start.' At first, I hardly dared to believe what she told me. But I thought it was worth a try. So I told God I was sorry for the past. I asked him to forgive me. And d'you know what happened? He forgave me. He washed me clean. He set me free from all that filth and evil. Even the guilt has gone. I didn't realise it was possible to be so happy. He's given me so much joy and I don't deserve it after what I've done.

That phrase, 'even the guilt has gone', never ceases to move me. Guilts are, among other things, the skeletons we stuff in the cupboard of our memory reminding us of failure and filling us with fear that, one day, the cupboard door could swing open and the skeletons fall in a heap at our feet. Guilt therefore produces an inner restlessness, a lingering dread that the past may yet catch up with us. The guilty person is at enmity with himself, with others and with God. Like Adam whose disobedience prompted him to hide from his wife by covering his nakedness with fig leaves as well as from the God who loved him (Genesis 3:6–10), guilt prevents us from celebrating our creativity and causes us, instead, to hide from ourselves, our nearest and dearest and from God.

The person who places their trust in God's loving plan of salvation, however, no longer needs to hide from their Creator or from others. Although our guilt and self-centredness once held us captive, God in Jesus paid the ransom which set us free from the legacy of the past. As Paul expressed the miracle to Titus: 'Our great God and Saviour, Jesus Christ . . . gave himself for us to redeem us from all wickedness' (Titus 2:13b,14a).

'To redeem' means to buy back or to buy. That is why, in the Book of Revelation, the redeemed celebrate the victory of the Lamb:

'You are worthy to take the scroll and to break its seals and open it: for you were slain, and your blood has bought people from every nation as gifts for God. (Revelation 5:9,LB).

In other words, God sees the skeletons in the cupboard, assures us that he loves us anyway and sets us free from their subtle control over our lives. He guarantees that the past has been dealt with and forgiven and he enables us to enter into the fullness of the abundant life he always intended us to enjoy.

Freedom from the sin-stained past

'Can this really be true? Can I really be forgiven?'

The speaker was a student friend of mine who needed to share the burden of the past with someone. He told me his story. When he was in the sixth form at school, like many young people today, he lived for number one, self. When he fell in love, he seduced his girl-friends on several occasions. Against all the odds, or so it seemed, one of them became pregnant. The child was adopted immediately after its birth. But Paul continued to shoulder the weight of the seriousness of this manifestation of self-centredness: the emotional scars he had inflicted on the girl and the responsibility of bringing an unwanted child into the world. Although it was past history he was describing and he had since responded to the love of God so that, in many ways he knew he was a new person, he continued to ask whether he could ever be sure of being free from *this*?

God has his own unique way of convincing people of the nature of his love and the answer to such questions, so we prayed together, asking him to give us a glimpse of what was in his Father-heart. God seemed to show Paul that the responsibility for the baby was now his and not Paul's. He also seemed to be promising to protect the baby's mother. As for Paul himself, the message of forgiveness which throbs through Luke 15 seemed to be applied specifically to him. In his imagination, he saw the heavenly Father running towards him, the prodigal determined to come home at last. And he felt the enfolding love of the God who embraced him. He wept. As tears of repentance and relief flowed, Paul sensed the mixture of emotions which welled up in God's heart: sorrow, unending love, tender forgiveness, to mention a few. And he knew that the past was forgiven. He could now entrust his son, his girl-friend and himself into God's unfailing love, walk resolutely away from the past and go free.

Undeserved? Yes. But that is what the grace of God is: undeserved love. Pure gift. Our former selves, our unregenerate life-style, our sinful past, our guilt: these were all pinned to the Cross of Christ crucified. They have no more hold over us. The failure which once made us blush, the back-log of guilt which once weighed us down, the sin which engulfed us like the tentacles of an octopus threatening to stifle our personality, have no more hold over us. Their power was destroyed the moment we trusted in Jesus's saving death.

Freedom from the penalty of sin

This is awesome. It is mystery. But equally awesome and mysterious are those words Jesus uttered from the Cross: 'It is finished.'

These words made a powerful impact on me while I was in the middle of writing this chapter. I was gazing at a crude wooden cross which someone had erected in the mountains where I was leading a retreat. As I gazed at the two pieces of wood which had been lashed together by a piece of rope and mounted on a pile of rocks, I spread before God a particular failure I wanted to leave with him. As I expressed my longing to be set free a triumphant roar seemed to come from the cross and echo round the mountain range: 'It is finished!' I was startled by the uncanny power with which those words seemed laced.

'What are you trying to say to me, Lord?' I asked.

The same words reached me with even greater force: 'It is finished.' And I wanted to weep because, suddenly, I knew what those words meant. My failure and I no longer belonged to one another. Jesus, by dying on a crude cross, had separated us. A severance had taken place, setting me free to be me once more. There would be no need to mention this failure to God again. Love for Jesus welled up in my heart reminding me of his claim that those who have been forgiven much, love much.

Because the love within me was so strong, I asked the Beloved to show me how he had felt as he hung nailed to the Cross and I tried, as it were, to step into his skin as he hung there. Whereupon a surge of joy filled me. I felt I understood why the prayer of the penitent thief, 'Jesus, remember me when you come into your Kingdom,' had elicited from Jesus a response of joy, strength and relief: 'Today you will be with me in Paradise.' Even though his body was being tortured, it gave Jesus joy to see that his agony was not in vain. One man, at least, was availing himself of the freedom for which he was paying such a phenomenal price.

Jesus could reassure the penitent because the word 'finished' is a legal word meaning 'accomplished'. It was often scrawled across bills in New Testament times. It means 'Paid!', 'Transaction completed!', 'Score settled!'

Like the thieves hanging either side of the Saviour, we have all offended our holy God in a whole variety of ways – not least by spurning his overtures of love and by refusing to allow God to be God. This is the essence of sin and, as Paul reminds us, 'the wages of sin is death' (Romans 6:23). But just as Jesus rescued the penitent, so he continues to rescue those who repent. Isaiah expresses the inexpressible:

We thought his troubles were a punishment from God, for his *own* sins! But he was wounded and bruised for *our* sins. He was chastised that we might have peace; He was lashed – and we were healed! *We* are the ones who strayed away like sheep. *We*, who left God's paths to follow our own. Yet God laid on *him* the guilt and sins of every one of us!

(Isaiah 53:4–6, LB).

In other words, because Jesus died on the Cross and rose again, we have been set free from the punishment which should have been ours. The judgment which should have been heaped on us, fell on him. In God's sight, it is as though, when Jesus died, we died with him so that God now looks on us as though we had never ever sinned. Our debt has been cancelled. Paid. We are free from sin's penalty. God has forgiven us.

When God forgives, he does not play a game of 'Let's pretend': 'Let's pretend they never sinned'. No. He sees us as we are: soiled, helpless, innately sinful. He knows what he is taking on when he promises to love us. Even so, he applies the righteousness of Jesus to us. When he looks on us, he sees, not the stain of the sin which has penetrated every particle of our being, but his pure and holy Son. It is as though we have been clothed in Jesus's own spotless, unsoiled garment. This is deep mystery. It can never be fully understood or fully explained – only contemplated with hearts bowed in adoration, love and praise as we recall that the freedom it bestows is instant. Irreversible. Complete. The penalty has been paid. God will not go back on this act. The deed is done.

Freedom from bondage

In order to appreciate the full extent of this amazing gift of grace, we need to place our personal short-comings in context and to recognise that, when the Bible uses the word 'sin,' it is not referring to acts of disobedience but rather to the world's orientation against God and towards self-centredness. This orientation governed Adam and Eve's life. Consequently, ever since the Fall, men and women have been in bondage to it. Body, mind and emotions have been snatched from their rightful owner, God, and enslaved by two terrorists: Satan and self.

A slave is a person who is owned by another; someone without rights who can be used, abused and disposed of in any way the owner chooses. A slave is compelled to obey his master. He has no right or power to say 'No' and no opportunity to express his God-given personality in the way it cries out to be expressed. But a slave's former owner has no more authority over him if he becomes someone else's property. He can no longer choke the former slave's potential.

The good news is that when we surrender to Christ, we are rescued from Satan and restored to our rightful owner: God. We are no longer forced to obey the dictates of the Prince of this world, the Evil One. Instead, we are set free to serve the One for whom we were made and to whom our hearts yearn to give glory: Christ our King. We are free to turn our backs on the temptation which peeps through the window of our life and beckons us. We are free to resist what Paul calls 'the ruling spirits of the universe . . . beings who are not gods' (Galatians 4:3, 8, GNB. We are free to bring glory to our Creator by discovering who it is he created us to be.

The chains which held us captive, the powers which once pushed us into self-centred practices, have no more hold over us. God in Christ has destroyed their stranglehold. The door to intimacy with God stands wide open. We are invited to call him Father, to approach him at any time and to enjoy to the full his peace. We are at one with him through the grace of atonement (at-one-ment). We are free indeed.

But, like Ron, with whom I began this chapter, we soon discover that that is not the whole story. Self still beckons. Sin still attracts. Satan still prowls seeking someone to devour. We are only partially free. As John Stott emphasises:

There is more to come . . . Christ 'gave himself to redeem us from all wickedness' (Titus 2:14), to liberate us from *all* the ravages of the Fall. This we have not yet experienced. Just as the Old Testament people of God, though already redeemed from their Egyptian and Babylonian exiles, were yet waiting for the promise of a fuller redemption, 'looking forward to the redemption

of Jerusalem', so the New Testament people of God,
though already redeemed from guilt and judgment, are
yet waiting for the 'day of redemption' when we shall be
made perfect.[2]

Ron had not yet appreciated this. By faith and theoretically,
he knew that, when he accepted Jesus as Lord and Saviour,
he had been set free to become the person God created him
to be. He did not know that when we commit ourselves to
Christ, we can commit to him only those parts of ourselves
with which we are consciously in touch. He had done that but
remained oblivious to the fact that these parts are only the
tip of the proverbial ice-berg. Deep within our subconscious
lie layer after layer of the hidden parts of ourselves. These
layers also need to be brought under the Lordship of Christ
because, though they lie dormant, their influence over us
for good or evil is immense. When Ron's eyes asked me
the question, 'Why am I not experiencing the freedom the
evangelist promises?' the question was rising, I suspect, from
one of these layers which, at that stage of his life, Ron did not
even know existed.

But since that Sunday twelve years ago, Ron has discovered
that entering into freedom in all its fullness, and watching our
true self emerge from its slavery to sin and self is a long-term,
life-long project. I sometimes liken it to the life-cycle of an
acorn. When an acorn is planted, its full potential is set free.
But the release is gradual: first one tiny, tentative root pokes
its nose out of the disintegrating shell into the dark earth.
Then another and another. Later, the first shoot pushes its
head through the soil into the light. All this growth is hidden
and even though it is steady and persistent, many years will
elapse before a fully mature, fruit-bearing oak tree will have
established itself.

In the chapters that follow, we examine ways of ensuring that
a similar miracle of growth takes place within each of us so that
our full, unique, God-implanted potential is gradually released
and we give glory to God by developing into the mature person
he created us to be.

For personal reflection

Read the following invitation from God:

> My child, let it be your privilege, each day, to dwell upon
> My sacrifice – made for the whole world.
> In My suffering love upon the Cross you see a *continuing
> process* . . . the unrequited love which pursues My children
> – yearning for the slightest response, and profoundly
> grateful when one of those children surrenders his or her
> life to Me.
> On the Cross, you see My heart of love crushed, for the
> moment, by the force of evil which darkens this universe.
> Then you see the bursting forth again of love's *power* . . .
> My Father's victory . . .
> Here, at the Cross, give Me your heart, anew, every
> day.[3]

Now, gaze at a cross or a picture of one. Ask yourself the
following four questions:

1. What is God saying through this Cross?
2. What is God saying *to me* through this Cross?
3. If I could step into the skin of the Saviour who died on that
   Cross, how might I feel about the world, the penitent thief,
   the by-standers and myself?
4. Write or say a prayer which sums up your response – or
   respond by drawing a picture or by writing a poem.

Notes for Chapter One

1. Here I am drawing on an insight quoted by John Stott in *The Cross
   of Christ* (Inter-Varsity Press, 1986). On p. 158 he describes a
   picture of the Crucifixion which hangs in an Italian church. In this
   picture a vast and shadowy Figure stands behind the figure of
   Jesus. The nail that pierces the hand of Jesus goes through to
   the hand of God. The spear thrust into the side of Jesus goes
   through into God's.

2. John Stott, *The Cross of Christ*, p. 178.
   I would recommend that any reader seeking a deeper understanding of the meaning of Christ's death should read and meditate on the contents of John Stott's book.
3. John Woolley, *I Am With You* (Crown, 1991) p. 3.

2

GRADUAL FREEDOM

Until we come to terms with the fact that God's gift of freedom comes as slowly and gradually as an acorn grows into an oak tree, we are in grave danger of growing disillusioned, we might even tie ourselves in knots of self-condemnation. Like Louise, a girl who once told me her story.

Louise is one of those effervescent Christians I described in the last chapter. She can vividly recall the time when she turned to Christ. She can even describe the exact place where she first sipped the nectar of instant freedom: 'It was a fantastic experience. I knew I was forgiven. I knew God had given me his Spirit. I felt a new and different person.'

Unfortunately, no one helped Louise to understand what freedom in Christ is and what it is not. When she came to see me three years after this dramatic spiritual experience, she confessed to feeling an abysmal failure: 'I really thought that Jesus had given me a completely new life – his life; that I wouldn't be tempted any more, that I was dead to sin, that I couldn't sin again. Then I met Steve. I fell in love with him. He wanted us to sleep together, so we did. I enjoyed it. It never occurred to me that there was anything wrong with it. But then a friend showed me Paul's teaching about sexual immorality[1] and now I've come to see that I'm a hopeless failure. Can God ever forgive me and set me free again?'

My heart went out to Louise. Why hadn't anyone taught her that although Jesus had set her free from her self-centred past, she was not hermetically sealed against sin forever? She was not free from the subtle wiles of Satan.[2] She was not free from temptation's apparent attractions.[3] She was not free from the desires of the flesh or of her old nature. Neither was she free from pain, struggle and the responsibility to make careful choices.

Christians who grow gradually into an awareness of the depth and height and length and breadth of God's love and who respond to that love over a period of time can also become as muddled as Louise. They can also be beguiled into believing that with God as their companion, they have been set completely free from all obstacles hindering their freedom.

Whether we respond to God's invitation to come to him through Jesus suddenly and spontaneously or slowly and after careful thought matters little. What does matter is that we understand what does and does not happen to us at this stage of our pilgrimage.

When we put our faith in Christ, it is true to say that we are translated from the kingdom of darkness into the kingdom of light. Peter assures us of this:

'God called you out of the darkness into his wonderful light' (1 Peter 2:9, LB).

It is also true to say that, though we were once God's enemies, now we are his friends. Paul says just that:

'We were God's enemies but he made us his friends through the death of his Son' (Romans 5:10, GNB).

And it is true that we have moved from death to life. These are unassailable Biblical truths.

But when we placed our trust in God's way of salvation, we did not leap-frog from an egocentric existence straight over the Cross and into God's glorious presence where sin ceases to exist and where suddenly we enjoy full maturity. Neither were we ejected from the kingdom of darkness straight into the new Jerusaiem, the world which revolves around God alone.

No. The Cross of Christ penetrated the prison walls which held us captive in the kingdom of darkness. The Cross of Christ also gave us access to God's Kingdom of light. But faith in Christ marks the beginning of the journey, not journey's end. The challenge which now faces us is to travel towards our goal, with Christ. He will accompany us along the path which leads to his Father and the new heaven and the new earth: the new

Jerusalem. Meanwhile there is a great deal of learning to do. We live life in the now, in 'the overlap',[4] the place where the old is restored, renewed and transformed, the place where we are being prepared to receive the new.

We have turned our back on the old life and walked away from it. We have walked, by way of Christ's Cross, towards that stage of the journey where all things will be, not only new, but perfect. But we have not yet reached our destination. We are pilgrims – travelling. We are pupils learning. We are children of the world, being changed so that we can take our place in the Kingdom of God – that Kingdom which, according to Jesus, is both a here and now reality: 'The kingdom of God is within you' (Luke 17:21), and a place we shall enjoy to the full in the future: 'I will not drink again of the fruit of the vine until the kingdom of God comes' (Luke 22:18).

Jesus nowhere uses the term 'the overlap' to describe the present. He does, however, tell parable after parable to help us to understand the nature and purpose of this in-between existence. These parables or metaphors appeal as much, if not more, to our imagination and emotions as to our intellects. They inform us on an intellectual level *and* on a deeper, emotional level also. This was deliberate on Jesus's part. Unlike twentieth-century Western scholars, Jesus did not teach through carefully crafted three-point sermons, through skilfully scripted papers which he proceeded to read to his audiences or even through careful exegesis of the Old Testament. On the contrary, he used stories, picture language, both to inform and *engage* his listeners. This way, he aimed to make an impact on every part of their personality: their minds and emotions, their imaginations and their wills.

The overlap: a place of gradual growth

Take the story of the sower, for example, a parable I frequently picture while I am on a particular prayer walk near my home in Cyprus. As I write, this walk takes me along paths which run beside newly ploughed fields – the kind of fields I imagine Jesus was surveying when he told the story of the 'farmer [who] went out to sow his seed' (Matthew 13:3). These fields are framed by sturdy thistles which wave in the wind, scattering their seeds far and near, reminding me of the picture Jesus paints of the seed that fell among thorns. The fields seem to be studded with impenetrable, sun-baked stones that would take months to remove, reminding me of the seed in Jesus's story which fell on stony ground. My attention is often attracted by the chattering and squawking of the birds that hop from furrow to furrow in the hope of finding tasty morsels. They remind me of the seed which was gobbled up before it could take root. Yet crops grow in these fields just as they did in Jesus's parable – not overnight, but slowly, gradually, persistently. The first sign of growth appears in the form of a green haze which seems to hover over the rich, red earth. Then sturdy little plants appear and, as these are kissed by the sun and watered by the irrigation system, they grow. Little by little, I have the thrill of witnessing a field full of crops and the joy and satisfaction which bring a proud smile to the face of the farmer.

As I walk and reflect, I sometimes try to imagine how Jesus's listeners would have reacted to this story and I am grateful to my friend and mentor Professor Kenneth Bailey for this insight:

'The Jews of the first century thought the Kingdom would come with a great apocalyptic revolution. The sun was going to be darkened, the land was going to give up its dead and there would be stars falling from the sky. In the middle of all this would come the Kingdom of God. But Jesus says no. The Kingdom of God comes like a seed quietly planted in the soil . . . There is no such thing as instant discipleship.[5]

And there is no such thing as instant maturity.

Louise, with whom I began this chapter, needed to have this message etched on her heart. Like many other young and not-so-young Christians today, she needed someone gently and patiently to explain to her that there is still no apocalyptic revolution which will result in her becoming a super-spiritual

Christian overnight. In God's economy and in God's Kingdom, we grow only gradually, just as we discover the nature of the person God created us to be only gradually.

The overlap: the place where we are transformed

Jesus painted another powerful pen-picture to underline this fact:

'The kingdom of heaven is like yeast that a woman took and mixed into a large amount of flour until it worked through the dough' (Matthew 13:33).

The implications of this parable were brought home to me in one of those powerful moments when God speaks through the marvels of his created world. I was in New Zealand at the time. My husband and I were visiting one of the wonders of the world: Milford Sound in Fiordland on the South Island. While my husband was buying tickets for the boat which was to take us out to the Tasman Sea via one of the fiords, I stood reading a plaque which described the nature of the water through which we would travel. The plaque informed me that there were two distinct layers of water: the top forty metres consisting of melted snow and providing a home for creatures who thrive in fresh water; and a hidden mass of salt water which never sees the sunshine but which provides a home for certain unique sea creatures.

'The fiord is rather like your life,' a still, small voice whispered. 'You also have an upper layer where you know God's Spirit is at work. You're naming and befriending the creatures which live in that layer. But there is another deep, hidden, mysterious layer which also needs to be owned and explored. Here live parts of your personality which you dismiss because they masquerade as monsters and appear to you grotesque yet these are also parts of your God-given personality which must be both named and befriended.'

The challenge travelled with me as I sat on the boat marvelling at the stunning beauty of the fiord and the mountains, the waterfalls and the water-life. It remains with me still and gives rise to a prayer that the Holy Spirit would, indeed, penetrate

every part of my being, transforming me into the likeness of
Christ and giving me the joy of ever-increasing maturity.

The overlap: a place of difficulty, tension and struggle

This transformation can only be slow and gradual, for, as Jesus's
parable of the sower clearly shows, there are many obstacles
to overcome. Although the heavenly sower has sown only
good seed into our lives, like a hungry, beady-eyed raven,
Satan watches where the seed falls and he is always ready
to pounce and snatch it away before it has time to take root.
Equally, times of testing and turbulence threaten to choke the
seed in the same way as thistles endanger the growth process.
Times of triumph and success may also stifle the embryonic life
of the plant. Despite these difficulties, the seed and the soil do
fuse and the result is lasting fruit. Jesus is at pains to assure
us that God does not give up on us. He uses the tempestuous
and joyful times to transform us into his likeness so that we are
ready to be presented mature in him when Jesus returns.

Paul also assures us that our eventual glorification is guaranteed. In his letter to the Romans he writes:

> God has shown us how much he loves us – it was while we
> were still sinners that Christ died for us! By his sacrificial
> death we are now put right with God . . . We were God's
> enemies, but he made us his friends through the death of
> his Son. Now that we are God's friends, how much more
> will we be saved by Christ's life!
>
> (Romans 5:8–10)

Commenting on this passage, John Stott observes:

> What the apostle means is surely this, that our developing,
> ripening Christian character is evidence that God is at work
> upon us and within us. The fact that God is thus at work

in our lives gives us confidence that He is not going to give up the job uncompleted. If He is working in us now to transform our character, He is surely going to bring us safely to glory in the end . . .

There is a strong presumption that we shall never be allowed to fall by the way, but shall be preserved to the end and glorified. This is not just sentimental optimism; it is grounded upon irresistible logic. The logic of it is this, that if, when we were enemies, God reconciled us through giving His Son to die for us, how much more, now we are God's friends, will He finally save us from His wrath by His Son's life? If God performed the more costly service (involving His Son's death) for His enemies, He will surely perform the less costly service now that His erstwhile enemies are His friends. Meditate on this until you see the irrefutable logic of Paul's argument.[6]

I once read a charming children's story which engraved these truths on my heart.

The heroine of the story is Yellow, a caterpillar who often dreamed of freedom but whose concept of the world of butterflies and flight was blurred and confused.

One day, when, as usual, thoughts of butterflies were occupying her caterpillar-brain, she came across a curious sight: a grey-haired caterpillar hanging upside-down on a branch. Seeing that he was caught in some kind of hairy stuff, Yellow offered her assistance.

'You seem in trouble . . . can I help?'

'No, my dear, I have to do this to become a butterfly.'

A butterfly! Yellow's caterpillar-heart leapt. Could this be her great opportunity?

'Tell me, sir, what is a butterfly?'

'It's what you are meant to become. It flies with beautiful wings and joins the earth to heaven . . .'

Yellow's heart somersaulted in hope. 'Me! A butterfly? It can't be true! . . . How can I believe there's a butterfly inside you and me, when all I see is a fuzzy worm?'

'How does one become a butterfly?' she added, pensive-
ly.

'You must want to fly so much that you are willing to
give up being a caterpillar.'

'You mean to die?' asked Yellow.

'Yes and no,' he answered. 'What *looks* like you will die
but what's *really* you will still live. Life is changed, not taken
away. Isn't that different from those who die without ever
becoming butterflies?'

'And if I decide to become a butterfly,' said Yellow
hesitantly, 'what do I do?'

'Watch me. I'm making a cocoon. It looks like I'm hiding,
I know, but a cocoon is no escape. It's an in-between house
where the change takes place. It's a big step, since you
can never return to caterpillar life. During the change, it
will seem to you or anyone who might peep that nothing is
happening – but the butterfly is already becoming. It just
takes time!'

Yellow was torn with anguish. What if she became this
thing called butterfly and her friends failed to recognize this
new self? At least she knew that caterpillars can crawl and
eat and love in a limited way. What happens if a caterpillar
gets stuck in a cocoon? Could she risk losing the only life
she had known when it seemed so unlikely she could ever
become a glorious winged creature? All she had to go on
was a caterpillar who believed sufficiently to take the leap
of faith. And hope.

The grey-haired caterpillar continued to cover himself
with silky threads. As he wove the last bit around his head
he called:

'You'll be a beautiful butterfly – we're all waiting for you!'
And Yellow decided to take the risk.

For courage she hung right beside the cocoon and began
to spin her own.

'Imagine, I didn't even know I could do this. That's
some encouragement that I'm on the right track. If I have
inside me the stuff to make cocoons – maybe the stuff of
butterflies is there too.'[7]

And, of course the stuff of butterflies *was* there. Yellow eventually emerged a brilliant, yellow, winged creature – a wonderful sight!

The overlap: a place of hope

There will be times in the overlap when, like Yellow, we are assailed with doubts; when we ask: 'How can I believe there's a butterfly inside me when all I see is a fuzzy worm?' Or, to put it another way: 'How can I believe God's Spirit is at work within me when all I see is a series of constant failures?'

There will be times when life in the overlap will seem as dull and drab and restricted as life in a cocoon; when we seem to be stripped of freedom rather than set free to enjoy life in all its fullness.

And there will be times when we seriously question whether the risk was worth taking; whether we have taken the first gigantic step along the pathway to God for no purpose; whether it would have been better to have remained in the kingdom of darkness than to respond to the finger which beckoned us to cross over into the Kingdom of Light.

But God is the Lord of the overlap. Even when our life seems of little value, even when we detect no spiritual movement, changes *are* taking place; the kind of changes which split open cocoons and produce butterflies. God is changing us. He has guaranteed to make us perfect in the end. He has guaranteed to set us free.

This makes our middle-world existence a place of hope. Hope in the Christian sense does not mean a vain longing. It means certainty. We do not hope for something we already possess. We anticipate it with eagerness, longing and gratitude. This hope motivates and energises us when the waiting seems endless, even futile.

Take the farmer in Jesus's parable, for example. As he scattered his seed, his heart was full of hope. In his imagination, almost certainly, he already saw a field full of wheat.

And what of the seeds he scattered? I was once given a

handful of mustard seeds – some of the smallest seeds in the world. As I held these tiny, black specks on the palm of my hand, I realised that I was holding a handful of hope, for surely, if seeds were sentient, and, like toys in the nursery in children's stories, could talk, they would be whispering to each other: 'I feel full of potential. I hope I'm sown in the kind of earth where a surge of life can flow through me, giving me the strength to push down long, white roots and to push up green shoots. I hope I become the tree I was intended to be.'

In a similar way, hope transforms us. As Henri Nouwen explains, hope influences the way we relate to God, the way we pray and the way we live. He contrasts the prayer of hope with 'the prayer of little faith', claiming that the person of little faith prays like a child who has asked Santa Claus for a present but who runs away frightened as soon as the present is placed into his hands: 'He would rather have nothing more to do with the old bearded gentleman. All the attention is on the gift and none on the one who gives it.'[8]

A person who hopes, on the other hand, prays differently. Their focus is not on the gift, but on the Giver. Their list of requests might be just as long as the list of the person of little faith, but ultimately their desire is not to receive answers to prayer but to affirm unlimited trust in the Giver of all good things.

In other words, hope is based on the belief that God gives only what is good.

Hope inspires an openness to God and his promises even though the way in which these promises will be fulfilled remains a mystery.

Hope sets us free to look at life through a new pair of spectacles.

As Henri Nouwen quoted:

Hope means to keep living
amid desperation
and to keep humming
in the darkness.
Hoping is knowing that there is love, . . .

In the midst of a gale at sea,
it is to discover land.
In the eyes of another
It is to see that he understands you.
Hope strengthens the awareness that everything we are
given and everything we are deprived of is nothing but a
finger pointing out the direction of God's hidden promise
which we shall taste in full.[9]

The overlap: the place where we deepen our relationship with God

Hope means to nurture a deep-down belief that God understands.

At the beginning of this chapter, I recalled the crisis of faith
which troubled Louise, the young Christian for whom hope had
almost died. Mine was the privilege of staying alongside her
until the embers of hope had been fanned into a flame. Mine
was the privilege of accompanying her a little further along the
pathway of faith. Mine was the joy of watching her discover for
herself that the overlap is not a place of sinless perfection but it
is a place where we may enjoy an ever-deepening relationship
with God.

She discovered this through meditating on Jesus's compelling
story of the son who squandered the inheritance entrusted to
him by his father. She could identify with this youth because,
like him, it was as a member of the family that she had failed.
Like him, she discovered that she had only to take one step
towards the heavenly Father to see that his arms were opened
to her in warmth and welcome and forgiveness. With relief
she ran into those arms and nestled there, rejoicing in God's
reconciling love. It was a humbling and tearful moment rather
than an ecstatic one. But it was life-changing to discover that,
even though she remains flawed, she is deeply loved.

That was twelve years ago. Since then she has experienced
the inevitable intertwining of joy and pain which life in the overlap
affords. She has also found out that the intimacy with God can

be an ongoing and ever-deepening experience. God loves us so much that he meets us where we are rather than demanding that we should be somewhere else. She knows now that, this side of eternity, she will always be vulnerable in the teeth of temptation. She also knows that prayer is a love relationship with God. God is not just her heavenly Father. He is her Friend and her Lover. And I have had the joy of watching her become ever more radiant as she absorbs this divine love. I have had the privilege of watching her become the loving, gifted, creative, compassionate person God created her to be.

For personal reflection

1. Imagine that you have been invited by a publisher to write your autobiography. Look back over your life and recall some of the major milestones – particularly in your journey with God. Write these down as though they were to form the chapter headings of your book. Then decide which incidents you would want to include under each heading. Notice as you do this exercise where your ability to be the person you were created to be has grown in leaps and bounds. Notice, too, where such growth has been slow and hidden.
2. Look back over the past twenty-four hours. Try to detect where God has been active in your life – in the good things and in the difficult circumstances. What do you sense God was attempting to say to you or show you about yourself, about God and about life?
3. Keep a journal, at least while you are reading this book. Write a letter to God in it in which you reflect on your journey through life so far. Write it from the heart.

Notes for Chapter Two

1. See, for example, 1 Corinthians 6:13; 1 Corinthians 6:18; 1 Corinthians 10:8; Ephesians 5:3; 1 Thessalonians 4:3, and my discussion of these verses in *Just Good Friends* (1985) and *Life in a Sex-Mad Society,* (1988) both published by Inter-Varsity Press.
2. See, for example, 1 Peter 5:8.

3. See, for example, Matthew 26:41; 1 Corinthians 10:13; 1 Timothy 6:9.
4. The 'overlap' is a term I first met in Jean Darnall's *Life in the Overlap* (Lakeland, 1977).
5. Here I am quoting from one of Professor Kenneth Bailey's videos: *Jesus, The Theologian: His Parables*. These are available from the Middle East Christian Organisation (MECO) and I would recommend them to anyone seeking a deeper understanding of the parables of Jesus.
6. John Stott, *Men Made New* (Inter-Varsity Press, 1966) pp. 15, 20.
7. Trina Paulus, *Hope for the Flowers* (Paulist Press, 1972).
8. Henri Nouwen, *With Open Hands* (Ave Maria Press, 1976) p. 80.
9. Henri Nouwen, *With Open Hands*, pp. 85, 86.

3

THE HOLY SPIRIT'S ROLE

The transformation of a person like Louise, whom I mentioned in the last chapter, bears the hallmarks of the ministry of the Holy Spirit. As Paul puts it, 'where the Spirit of the Lord is, there is freedom' (2 Corinthians 3:17). Or as Jesus expresses it, the Holy Spirit, the agent of truth, is the One who will lead us into the truth which will set us free (John 14:17 and 16:13). To proceed further in our exploration of how we become the people God always intended us to be without further reference to the Holy Spirit would therefore be as foolish and irresponsible as the way the harvesters looked in a mental picture which God seemed to give to a certain pastor on one occasion.

While the pastor was praying, he saw a mental video which seemed to carry with it the kind of revelatory message which characterised the vision Peter saw while he was praying on the rooftop in Acts 10:9. The pastor saw, not a sheet being let down to earth by its four corners, but a group of harvesters gathering golden grain from a farmer's field. But as the pastor looked at the sequence of pictures closely and carefully, he observed that the workers were using not farming implements but spoons. As the short film continued to play on the screen of his mind, it became apparent that there was no need for their progress to be hampered in this way because parked on a road adjacent to the field stood a farm wagon which was loaded with harvesting tools: sickles, rakes and pitch-forks.

Just as Peter's vision was used by the Holy Spirit to change his perception of Gentiles, so God used this pastor's picture to persuade him that it is possible to attempt to do God's work with the inadequate tools of our own abilities and insights or it is possible to avail ourselves of the Holy Spirit's gifts: among others, his wisdom and counsel and power.

I heard this pastor describe his 'vision' to a group of Tanzanian clergy, including bishops. Since many of them spoke little or no English, one of the Tanzanian bishops translated the experience into Swahili and I still remember him breaking into peals of laughter as he saw, in his mind's eye, the absurdity of the picture: a group of grown-ups harvesting a whole field with small spoons.

Who the Holy Spirit is

It is equally absurd for us to embark on the life-long journey of becoming the person God created us to be without calling on the assistance of God's Spirit to help us. Jesus did, after all, call him the Helper. Yet many of us shun the Holy Spirit's involvement in the process of self-discovery. There are many reasons for this. One is fear. As someone expressed it to me just before I began to write this chapter: 'I've realised that I'm scared of the Holy Spirit. I don't think of him as a person, I think of him as a thing and I avoid reading the Acts of the Apostles because much of it seems weird.'

I, too, used to fear the Holy Spirit's ministry and consequently erected seemingly impenetrable barriers against his intervention in my life. I, too, used to harbour a secret store of doubts about the desirability of opening my life to the 'Holy Ghost', as the Holy Spirit used to be called in the Book of Common Prayer and the Authorised Version of the Bible on which I was reared as a child, so I sensed I understood some of the reasons why this person trembled when the Holy Spirit was mentioned.

When I investigated my own ambivalence towards the third person of the Holy Trinity, I realised that two main factors contributed to it. One covered the excesses and eccentricities of some of the so-called Spirit-filled Christians known to me at then. The other was some of the teaching on the Holy Spirit and his activity which I had received as a child and as a young adult.

I think, for example, of that terrifying word 'ghost' which seemed designed to drive people from the Holy Spirit rather than encourage them to draw near. Or words like 'wind' and 'fire' which my Sunday School teachers had used to help us to understand the Holy Spirit's activity in our lives. Such words had conjured up in my childish mind the fires caused by enemy shelling during the Second World war; fires which had gutted the magnificent cathedral in our city; and fires which had demolished people's homes and business premises, plunging the young and the elderly alike into inexpressible grief and despair. Having witnessed these catastrophes as a child, I wanted nothing to do with God's fire.

Similarly the word 'wind', which describes the Spirit, came to me laced with negative overtones. It would remind me of a poem I learned in school which contrasted the beauty and warmth of the sun with the mischievous, unpredictable behaviour of the wind. It would remind me, too, of the howling wind which would sometimes bite into me while I walked to school or church. The word caused me to recoil from the wind of God's Spirit. And even as an adult, the term 'the empowering Spirit' sounded warning bells inside me. The phrase reminded me of verses describing seemingly wild, uncontrolled and uncontrollable behaviour:

'The Spirit of the Lord came upon [Samson] in power so that he tore the lion apart with his bare hands as he might have torn a young goat. But he told neither his father nor his mother what he had done' (Judges 14:6).

Such violence and deceit repelled me. Consequently I distanced myself from the Holy Spirit and developed a strong dislike of the word 'power'. This dislike deepened in the early 1960s when many seemingly eccentric Christians claimed to have been endued with power from the Holy Spirit. 'If this is power', I concluded, 'I don't want it.' I turned my back on the Holy Spirit because, in the circles in which I then moved, what passed for power communicated itself to me as little more than brashness and the extremes of extrovert enthusiasm. My ambivalence deepened because those who claimed to be Spirit-filled always dressed in T-shirts bearing the slogan: 'Smile, God loves you' and a transfer of a 'smiley face'. They called their spiritual effervescence joy and, when challenged, were quick to claim that their behaviour was Biblical. They would point to verses like 1 Samuel 10:5–7 where we read of Saul encountering and being influenced by a procession of zealous men playing lyres and tambourines, flutes and harps, and praising God in exuberant fashion. The defendants of this kind of religious fervour seemed totally unaware that someone else's religious euphoria could communicate itself to others as an objectionable lack of balance.

Although I rejected the enthusiasm which masqueraded as power, I detected within myself a deep-down hunger – even an envy as, slowly, over a period of some eight years, I discerned that people whose availability to the Holy Spirit was genuine seemed somehow to change. The only way I can describe the subtlety of what I observed was that they became a richer expression of their former selves.

This set me on a quest. I would probe into questions like: 'Who is this Holy Spirit? What is its ministry?'

The Holy Spirit: a person

The first thing I discovered was that, although the Holy Spirit *is* frequently referred to as wind, water and fire, the Bible makes it quite clear that, first and foremost, he is a person. As Jesus puts it, he is a counsellor, a comforter, and an advocate.[1] He guides us[2] and speaks to us,[3] convinces and constrains us,[4] transforms and warns us.[5] He can be grieved[6] and lied against.[7] Moreover, he is not just any person. He is the third person of the Holy Trinity who, from all eternity, has emanated from God the Father and God the Son. As someone has summarised the situation: 'He is the uncreated, creative power of the holy, loving God. He is personally present to but transcendently other than the human spirit.'[8] Paul goes so far as to call him, not only God's Spirit (2 Corinthians 3:3) but God himself (2 Corinthians 3:17). His presence is made known to us by Jesus who refers to him as the Father's good gift (Luke 11:13).

'The Father's good gift.' Certainly, the words Jesus chooses conjured up 'good' pictures. The 'advocate' had special meaning for me at this time. A few months earlier, my husband and I had been involved in a car crash in what was then Yugoslavia. Because I had sustained back and head injuries I became a patient for a week in a primitive hospital. Meanwhile my husband was left with the arduous task of trying to salvage our belongings from the wrecked car, look after our two young children, sort out our financial affairs and try to deal with the legal wranglings surrounding the crash. He would have been totally unable to cope without the help of the village advocate – a man who befriended us and took a great deal of care and trouble to acquaint himself with our plight but who was also fully conversant with the law of the land; a man who could therefore be the go-between in whom the local legal system and our family met and understood each other.

According to William Kelly, this is precisely what the Holy Spirit does. As our Advocate, he identifies with our interests, undertakes our cause, covenants to see us through all our difficulties and becomes our Representative before God. At the same time he is Jesus's Representative. He makes Jesus present to us and reveals all that Jesus is to us. He secures for us all that the Father has to give. He is the One who brings Jesus to us and us to Jesus.[9]

Even though these insights allayed some of my fears, I was startled by Jesus's claim: 'It is better for you that I go away, because if I do not go, the Helper will not come to you. But if I do go away, then I will send him to you' (John 16:7, GNB).

Like many other Christians, there are so many times in my life when I envy the disciples the privilege that was theirs of encountering Jesus face to face when he walked this earth. I, too, would have dearly loved to have seen and heard him, touched him and been held by him. I, too, would have loved to have watched him at work and listened to him pray. 'But no,' he seems to say. 'It is for your good that you cannot see or hear me in the flesh. It is in your best interests that I go away. It is to your advantage that, instead, I infuse you with my Holy Spirit.'

This caused me to question whether the claim that the Holy Spirit is Jesus's Alter Ego – Jesus's 'other self' – might be correct; that this is the reason why it is better for us that the God-man Jesus returned to his Father so that he could come to us in a different guise. If this was true, I reasoned, and it is also true that the Holy Spirit is the breath, the energy and the personality of Jesus, do I not need to do a U-turn and face him rather than flee from him? If it is true that, when the Spirit in-breathes us, little by little, we become more like Jesus, this is another reason why I should draw closer to him rather than run from him. We are created in the image of God and if the Holy Spirit can help me to become more like Jesus, to have him permeating my life is a necessity not a luxury.

The Holy Spirit: a lovely person

The thought challenged me – especially in the light of Galatians 5:22 where Paul spells out the nature of the fruit the Holy Spirit causes to mature in the believer: love and joy, peace and patience, kindness and goodness, faithfulness, gentleness and self-control.

Joy, I reflected, is the ability to rejoice in spite of irksome circumstances, trying people or persistent pain. Love is the unselfish affection which always seeks to promote the well-being of others attempting to meet their deepest needs and facilitate their growth. Peace is the ability to remain calm, tranquil and serene in every circumstance because we entrust all things to the wisdom, sovereignty and omniscience of God, while a patient person keeps on enduring those things they do not enjoy and also accepts people's weaknesses. Gentleness means the ability to place ourselves in another's shoes and so to identify with their feelings and circumstances that we inflict no needless pain on them. Gentleness increases in us the ability to dispense with rudeness, harshness or abrasiveness. Even when the gentle person needs to be firm, the firmness comes laced with compassion, tenderness and the self-control without which these qualities would be impossible.

I understand goodness to mean the rejection of all that is not of God. It is that quality which allows God to be God in our lives. Faithfulness is the loyalty, reliability, dependability and commitment which never disappoints and never lets another down; the quality which can assure another, 'When I say I'll be your friend, I'll always be your friend.' Self-control is the ability to hear the clamour of one's own rebel emotions and inner needs, coupled with the skill to know which to discipline, as we would control an unruly class of children, and which to meet. Like Jesus, the self-controlled person enjoys the inner harmony which stems from a body, mind and soul in perfect working order. And humility was once described to me as that art whereby, when we know we have done something well, we give the glory to God and keep a little bit of encouragement for ourselves.

I remember reading and being beckoned by Robert Frost's reflection on the One who causes this fruit to mature in us:

'Only a *lovely* person can minister *love* . . . Only a *joyful* person can minister *joy* . . . Only a *peaceful* person can minister *peace* . . . Only a *hopeful* person can minister *hope*.'[10]

As I turned this claim over in my mind, I felt further drawn to the Holy Spirit and his ministry. And when I reflected on the way he brooded like a protective bird over the chaos which gradually became the wonderful world of Genesis 1 and 2, the fear in my heart melted and was replaced by awe. This sense of awe increased when, in Psalm 104, I noticed that it is the Holy Spirit who constantly renews the heavens and the earth, the sea and the rivers, the mountains, the moon and the sun, together with all living creatures: birds, plants, trees and the whole of mankind.

Awe was strengthened when I meditated on the Holy Spirit's role in the conception, birth and public ministry of Jesus. It seemed to me that his role had been, in part, an administrative one and, like any good administrator, he had ensured that everything dovetailed together smoothly so that necessary changes could take place as effectively and painlessly as possible.

And fear was further dispelled when I read Jesus's claim that this transforming, life-giving Spirit who inspired the 'letter from home' which is so precious to me (2 Peter 1:21), always glorifies the Son and promotes his Lordship.[11]

So, since John records that Jesus breathed his Spirit into his disciples, and since Luke recalls how the disciples were overwhelmed by the Spirit on the Day of Pentecost, and since John promised that Jesus would likewise 'baptise', that is, clothe, overshadow or immerse believers with his Spirit, I began to pray, in the words of the chorus:

> Spirit of the Living God,
> Fall afresh on me . . .
> Melt me, mould me, fill me, use me,
> Spirit of the living God fall afresh on me.
> (My version of a familiar chorus)

That was twenty years ago. With the wisdom of hindsight, I sense I can trace some of the ways in which this lovely, third member of the Holy Trinity has been and still is putting me in touch with the person God always created me to be. I discovered, too, that he is showing me some of the characteristics of true, enfleshed freedom. Like Billy Graham, I have drawn the conclusion that 'I need Jesus Christ for my eternal life, and the Holy Spirit of God for my internal life'.[12]

Filled with the Spirit

Before I could discover experientially the precise nature of the Holy Spirit's ministry, however, my eyes were to be opened to the meaning of Paul's injunction to 'be filled with the Spirit' (Ephesians 5:18).

One of the first clues I found seemed a curious one. To enter into the fullness of the freedom God grants and to become the person he always intended us to be, we must surrender ourselves to him. George Matheson sums up this paradox in the first two lines of his well-loved hymn:

> Make me a captive, Lord,
> And then I shall be free.

The Holy Spirit who has been variously described as the Advocate or the Go-Between God or the best man who introduces the Bridegroom (Christ) to the Bride (his church), facilitates this liberating process. He does it, in the words of Paul, by flooding our hearts with God's love (Romans 5:5, JBP).

Will I ever forget the evening when, in a friend's lounge, God gave me the graced moment where I was able to experience this for myself? The friend in whose home it happened had telephoned me to say that he believed he had been baptised with the Holy Spirit and that he had begun to pray in tongues. Still struggling between a desire to be open to the Spirit of God and a disdain for the eccentricities I have already described, my initial response was: 'Oh dear! Maybe we can talk about it on Monday after the meeting.'

The meeting had finished, everyone else had gone home and my friend had told me his story. The genuineness of his experience touched me and although I had gone to the meeting fully intending to 'sort him out' theologically, I knew that to dispute what he had told me would be an affront to him, a trusted friend, and to God. Instead, I simply reverenced his story.

As we had done so often before, we then prayed together. As we prayed, I became aware of him gently and quietly praying in tongues. I became aware, too, at one stage, that he was laying his hands on my head very gently and asking God to touch me afresh. No rushing wind swept through the room and no tongues of flame hovered over our heads but gradually the lounge became holy ground as the sense of the presence and the love of God overshadowed me. As I reflected on this later, it was as though God was pouring into me liquid love. I could almost feel it being spread through every cell of my brain before it percolated round the inner recesses of my being. The sensation stunned me, silenced me and thrilled me. When I left my friend's home and walked through the dark streets to my own, the love seemed to intensify and as I slipped into bed beside my husband, the love continued to overshadow and to overwhelm me. So far as I am aware, sleep eluded me that night but I was glad of the hushed darkness to absorb the elixir of love in a way I had never before envisaged, let alone experienced.

For days, although I carried on with my normal routine, I seemed strangely detached from it all. It was as though I was watching the world through double-glazed windows. Outside, my family and friends were acting normally; inside, I felt as though as I was moving in a womb of love.

'I suppose this is what people call being "baptised with the Holy Spirit",' I said to my husband. He understood, though neither of us appreciated what we now know – that, as Andrew Murray described it one hundred years ago:

'The Spirit is nothing less than the Divine Love itself come down to dwell in us . . . The Spirit comes to us freighted with all the love of God and of Jesus: the Spirit is the Love of God . . . The outpouring of the Spirit is the inpouring of Love.'[13]

When this love-shedding Spirit not only indwells us but also immerses us in love, he gives far more than the head-knowledge that God loves us intimately and uniquely. In Paul's words, he spreads God's love into the nooks and crannies of our lives until, in that love, we live and move and have our entire being.

He convicts us of sin

This love with which God loves Jesus, ourselves and all his children, now possesses our hearts and draws from us a reciprocal love. At least, that was my experience. Love and praise welled up inside me as from a well-supplied fountain. Whether I was praying or washing up, worshipping or fetching the children from school, the cool, coloured waters sprang spontaneously from the fountain within, and mingled with the liquid love of God which continued to flow into me and refresh me. 'But why did I have to wait so long for this?' I once asked God.

For a whole year I had prayed from the poverty of my parched and hungry heart that God would meet me in the spiritual desert in which I had been wandering. I had anticipated that, in answer to this prayer, water would flow from the mountain top into the caked clay of my soul, saturate me, fill me and create within me an oasis where fresh flowers could blossom, where birds would sing and where butterflies of every colour and hue would dance to the music of the spirit.

Instead, for a whole year, I pleaded: 'Lord, drench me with the water of your Holy Spirit if that's what I need,' but no water came – only increased barrenness and the awareness that the emptiness inside me was growing steadily bigger and more cavernous.

'I was preparing you,' he seemed to whisper. And, at last, I understood.

Throughout this year, a horrifying awareness of my own sinfulness crept over me so that I saw myself as I really was: a sinner, coated with grime. I am not implying that the cause of *all* spiritual dryness is sin. It is not. Often it is a gift from God causing us to cry out for a fresh touch of the Spirit. On this occasion, though, I was brought face to face with my innate sinfulness.

It wasn't that I had committed any of the spectacular sins like adultery or murder or theft. Ordinary, humdrum, grubby little sins had accumulated, encrusting me without my noticing. After all, I had been too busy *serving* God to be over-conscious of sin. But during this year, I saw it and felt cheated. Where was the promised energising that the Holy Spirit was supposed to inject (Acts 1:8)? I remember protesting: 'Lord, I asked you for more of your Spirit's life and power. All you have given me is an awareness of sin; not even anyone else's sin. My own!' Now the truth appeared in rather the same way as the rising sun peeps over the mountain range opposite our home ushering in a new day of hope and promise. God *had* been answering my heart-cry, 'Drench me with your Spirit', but he had answered it in a way I had not anticipated or understood because I had not appreciated Jesus's warning that one of the Holy Spirit's main tasks is to convict the world of sin (John 16:8).

Theologians advise us that the word 'convict' was the word customarily used for the cross-examination of a witness or a man on trial. It always carries with it the concept of a cross-examination *process* in that the trial continues until the person admits his wrong-doing.[14] In other words, when the Holy

Spirit permeates and penetrates our innermost beings, he shines
the torch of his truth on the inconsistencies which prevent us
from becoming the loving and lovable people God created us to
be. His purpose in exposing them is not to condemn or to crush
us but rather gently to reveal to us how self mars God's image
in us, dishonours him and short-changes our personalities. His
further purpose is to bring us to that point where we beg him
to continue in us his sanctifying work (2 Thessalonians 2:13).
But, as the writer of the Epistle to the Hebrews warns us, to be
disciplined in this way always feels disconcerting and humiliating
rather than consoling.

The scene which greets me as I gaze out of my study window
has become, for me, a parable of this aspect of the Holy Spirit's
ministry. The vineyards and orange and lemon groves in the
valley below bask in the warm sunshine and stretch out to
touch the aquamarine Mediterranean sea. The arms of the
pampas grass wave in the wind while a blue haze partly masks
the mountains which frame the picture. But today this beauty
is somewhat marred by a vast expanse of black, scorched
land. Two days ago, these terraces were a blond tangle of
tall, dried grasses and shoulder-high, unruly weeds. Then, as
is the custom at this time of year, a fire was lighted to purge
the area of pests and undergrowth. And although the pocked
landscape still looks charred, already I am reaping some of the
benefits of this seemingly ruthless and dangerous operation.
Displaced birds are perching on the branches of the trees in
our garden, regaling us with their song and delighting us with
the luxuriance of their brightly coloured wings. The path from
our home which had been completely overgrown is now not only
visible, but usable. And the field rats which were beginning to
venture from the field into our house have been driven away.

This parable of nature reminds me that the Holy Spirit's task
of purging us of sin is designed, not to humiliate or to destroy
us, but rather to set us free from all that would pollute us and
mask the Christ-like qualities God has invested in us. The
Holy Spirit's part in this double exposure of our sin and our
giftedness is crucial. Since he is the one who equipped us to
serve God in the first place, he is the one who is most capable

of helping us discover precisely the kind of person he created us to be.

He equips us

This aspect of the Holy Spirit's ministry is highlighted in Exodus 31:3–5 where God says of Bezalel:

'I have filled him with the Spirit of God, with skill, ability and knowledge in all kinds of crafts – to make artistic designs for work in gold, silver and bronze, to cut and set stones, to work in wood, and to engage in all kinds of craftsmanship.'

I sometimes wonder how long it took Bezalel to discover that his seemingly natural talents were, in fact, indications of the kind of person God always intended him to be; whether his exploration into self-awareness was as long and difficult as ours sometimes is. We are not told. What we are told is that we cannot make such discoveries on our own. As William Temple once observed:

It is no good giving me a play like *Hamlet* or *King Lear*, and telling me to write a play like that. Shakespeare could do it: I can't. And it is no good showing me a life like the life of Jesus and telling me to live a life like that. Jesus could do it: I can't. But if the genius of Shakespeare could come and live in me, then I could write plays like that. And if the Spirit of Jesus could come and live in me, I could live a life like that.[15]

If the Spirit of Jesus could come? The good news is that the sanctifying Spirit of Jesus *has* come. He hovers over our chaos and inner darkness and, when we give him the go-ahead, gradually reveals to us and connects us with the person God created us to be.

'When we give him the go-ahead.' The way to give him the go-ahead is to heed Paul's injunction to 'be filled with the Spirit' (Ephesians 5:18). One prerequisite for being filled with the Spirit, as I have already indicated, is to acknowledge our need and inner emptiness. As Andrew Murray shrewdly observes:

'The first condition of all filling is emptiness. What is a reservoir but a great hollow, a great emptiness prepared, waiting, thirsting, crying for the water to come?'[16]

Another prerequisite is spelt out by Jesus when he exhorts us to ask:

> 'Ask and it will be given to you; seek and you will find . . . Which of you fathers, if your son asks for a fish, will give him a snake instead? Or if he asks for an egg, will give him a scorpion? If you then, though you are evil, know how to give good gifts to your children, how much more will your Father in heaven give the Holy Spirit to those who ask him?
>
> (Luke 11:9–13)

A third prerequisite is openness to be filled with God's Spirit in whatever way God chooses to in-breathe us.

Like me, countless Christians have discovered that God impregnated them with his Spirit in great gentleness, while the Holy Spirit has come to others in a far more dramatic way. While recognising the authenticity of both and while allowing God to be God in every situation, giving him the spaciousness to enrich our lives in whatever way he chooses, we need to heed Andrew Murray's warning when he observes that the sudden, mighty manifestations of the Holy Spirit, which result in an over-dependence on the fellowship, sometimes have a tendency towards superficiality. The experience reaches the upper, most accessible parts of our personality but leave the hidden depths of the inner life and the current of our will untouched and unchanged. When this happens, our journey towards maturity and our struggle to discover the person God created us to be suffers a set-back. We therefore need constantly to be aware that what is required is not just a past testimony, whether that testimony bears witness to a sudden or gradual conversion experience or an immersion in God's Spirit. No. What is needed is the regular, daily, hourly, ongoing infilling of the Holy Spirit whose further task it is to enlighten us as we feast on God's Word as well as to teach us to pray – the topics on which we shall focus in the next four chapters.

For personal reflection

1. Take a few minutes to still yourself in the presence of God.
2. Read John 20:19–23. Re-read it until you are really familiar with the details of this account of the first Easter Day.
3. Picture the scene as vividly as you can.
4. Now step into the picture so that you are there with the disciples. Notice who is there, what the atmosphere in the room is like, how you feel about being there and where you place yourself – in the middle of the group, for example, or hiding in a corner.
5. Watch the disciples' reactions as Jesus enters the room despite the locked doors. Let the rest of the story unfold and become involved in it – doing as Jesus suggests: gazing at his hands and his side.
6. Be aware that he is breathing his Spirit into the disciples. And he approaches you. Register how it feels to have him close enough to breathe on you. Register, too, how you feel about him breathing his Spirit into you. Are you resisting? Or receiving?
7. Write him a prayer telling him the thoughts and emotions which are clamouring for attention inside you.

Notes for Chapter Three

1. John 14:16 (where the word 'Counsellor' is variously translated 'Comforter' and 'Advocate').
2. Nehemiah 9:19,20; Luke 4:1
3. 2 Samuel 23:2;2 Peter 1:21
4. Acts 13:4
5. Nehemiah 9:30
6. Isaiah 63:10
7. Acts 5:3.
8. *The New Bible Dictionary* (Inter-Varsity Press, 1980) p. 534.

9. William Kelly, quoted by Andrew Murray in *The Spirit of Christ* (Anson D.F. Randolph and Company, New York, 1888) p. 356.
10. Robert Frost, *Set My Spirit Free* (Logos, 1973) p. 39.
11. John 16:14.
12. Billy Graham, *The Holy Spirit* (Fount, 1978) p. 12.
13. Andrew Murray, *The Spirit of Christ*, p. 283.
14. William Barclay, *John's Gospel: The Daily Study Bible* (Saint Andrew Press, 1955).
15. William Temple, quoted by John Stott in *Basic Christianity* (IVP, 1971) p. 102
16. Andrew Murray, *The Spirit of Christ*, p. 306.

4

THE PLACE OF PRAYER

Superficiality and the quest to discover our true identity in Christ are incompatible. As Christians we are called, not to remain shallow, but rather to respond in the deep places of our personality to the deep love of God. That, at least, is the way I understand the Psalmist's phrase, 'deep calls to deep' (Psalm 42:7).

Often, when I lead prayer retreats and Quiet Days, I find people using this phrase of the Psalmist as a prayer: 'May the hidden depths of my being be touched by the depths of your love, Lord.' That is why the Holy Spirit's involvement in our life is so important. As Paul reminds us, the 'Holy Spirit speaks to us *deep* in our hearts' (Romans 8:16, LB, my emphasis). He not only speaks, he helps. In his role as Counsellor or Comforter, he is fully qualified to draw alongside us whenever we are in any kind of need for help.

Prayer is one of the areas into which he delights to move. This is good news because prayer, of all places, is the forum where we discover who and what God created us to be.

By prayer, in this chapter, I am not referring to petitionary prayer or intercessory prayer, nor to spiritual warfare or the prayer of confession, vital though these and other facets of the jewel of prayer are in the life of the believer. I am thinking solely of that aspect of prayer which is an ever-deepening relationship with God. Richard Foster labels this the prayer of home-coming, the prayer which becomes the place where 'we come home to where we belong'.[1] It is the place where we 'come home to that for which we were created',[2] 'the place of deepest intimacy, where we know and are known to the fullest'.[3] This prayer is 'a love relationship: an enduring, continuing, growing love relationship with the great God of the universe'.[4]

The prayer of Jesus

This is the kind of prayer into which Jesus drew his disciples when he called them to 'Come with me by yourselves to a quiet place and get some rest' (Mark 6:31). It is the kind of prayer into which he woos us today.

The context of the original invitation fascinates me. The disciples had just returned from the mission to the villages on which they had been sent by Jesus. It would appear that it had been fruitful. But such missions are draining, as Jesus well knew from personal experience so, instead of sending them straight back into another campaign, he gave them the opportunity of rest, in a quiet place, with him.

Did the disciples protest that there were so many souls to be saved, so many people needing healing, so many others to be delivered from oppression, that to spend time with the Master would be pure self-indulgence? I doubt it. They were well acquainted with his own rhythm of prayer which included frequent forays into the hills where he could be alone with his Father. They knew that when he returned from such times in the Father's presence, he seemed re-energised, empowered and full of wisdom and purpose as though the Father had given him the next piece of the map to guide him on the next phase of the journey. Surely they would have reasoned that, if prayer in a quiet place could re-charge the Master's batteries, it could re-charge theirs also? Jesus not only retreated frequently to quiet places where his relationship with his Father could be nurtured, he applauded Mary of Bethany for turning her back on the tyranny of the urgent in favour of spending leisurely time at the feet of her Beloved, and he gently rebuked Martha for failing to discern the one thing necessary (Luke 10:42).

The place where we know ourselves loved

Why was it that Jesus removed himself from the thronging crowds to spend quality time with his Father? What drew him from his bed to spend the early hours of the morning on the hushed shores of the sea of Galilee? What prompted him to spend the entire night under the star-studded sky?

Do we not find a clue in Matthew 3:17?

The occasion is Jesus's Baptism. His public ministry has not yet begun. The crowds have not yet recognised him as the miracle worker. The Twelve have not yet been called to live in community with him. Yet, as Jesus rises from the waters of the Jordan to face the people he already loved, his Father's cry from heaven echoed round the Jordan valley: 'This is my Son, whom I love; with him I am well pleased' (Matthew 3:17). In other words, the Father seems to be underlining that his Son was uniquely loved not for anything he had achieved but simply for who he was. When we become aware of such love, it not only motivates us for ministry, it reminds us that we are loved, not for what we do but for who we are. It reminds us, as someone has put it, that we were created to be human *beings* and not human *doings*.

The Father's love so energised Jesus that he wanted his disciples to know themselves loved also. That, surely, is the reason why he invited them to escape from the crowds which clamoured so persistently that Jesus and his friends had no time to eat? That, surely, is the reason why he applauded Mary for her foresight and intuitive knowing that when she sat at his feet she was in the right place? That, surely, is the reason why he still pleads with us: '*You* come aside *with me* and get some rest'?

We need to notice that the invitation is not simply to take a break. No. The invitation is to take a holiday with him. Henri Nouwen explains the reason that this emphasis is so crucial to our quest to discover precisely who it is God created us to be. His thesis is that the words 'You are my Beloved' 'reveal the most intimate truth about all human beings'[5] and that 'being

the Beloved expresses the core truth of our existence'.[6] He
goes on to ask:

> Aren't you, like me, hoping that some person, thing or
> event will come along to give you that final feeling of inner
> well-being you desire? Don't you often hope: 'May this
> book, idea, course, trip, job, country or relationship fulfill
> my deepest desire.' But as long as you are waiting for that
> mysterious moment you will go on running helter-skelter,
> always anxious and restless, always lustful and angry,
> never fully satisfied . . .
>
> Well, you and I don't have to kill ourselves. We are the
> Beloved. We are intimately loved long before our parents,
> teachers, spouses, children and friends loved or wounded
> us. That's the truth of our lives. That's the truth I want
> you to claim for yourself. That's the truth spoken by the
> voice that says, 'You are my Beloved.'
>
> Listening to that voice with great inner attentiveness,
> I hear at my center words that say, 'I have called you
> by name, from the very beginning. You are mine and I
> am yours. You are my Beloved, on you my favor rests.
> I have molded you in the depths of the earth and knitted
> you together in your mother's womb. I have carved you in
> the palms of my hands and hidden you in the shadow of my
> embrace. I look at you with infinite tenderness and care for
> you with a care more intimate than that of a mother for her
> child. I have counted every hair of your head and guided
> you at every step. Wherever you go, I go with you, and
> wherever you rest, I keep watch . . . You belong to me
> . . . We are one.'
>
> Every time you listen with great attentiveness to the
> voice that calls you the Beloved, you will discover within
> yourself a desire to hear that voice longer and more deeply.
> It is like discovering a well in the desert. Once you have
> touched wet ground you want to dig deeper.[7]

Prayer is the place where we discover, not simply a well, but
an oasis. The prayer which is a relationship with God is the place

where we hear God say to *us*, 'You are my Beloved.' And, as Henri Nouwen concludes:

'From the moment we claim the truth of being the Beloved, we are faced with the call to become who we are. Becoming the Beloved is the great spiritual journey we have to make.'8

The place where we are re-created

But, in order that we might be set free to 'claim the truth of being the Beloved', we need to be re-created or, in New Testament terms, to be born again. That is not as difficult or nonsensical as it sounded to Nicodemus to whom Jesus first used the term. The prayer which is a developing relationship with God can become the womb where, gradually, God sets us free to become the people he always intended us to be.

This theory became a beautiful reality for me one Good Friday. I was leading a retreat at the time and, while the group were having lunch, I went to look at the simple cross one of the other leaders had created with two branches she had found in the garden. As I gazed at this makeshift cross, at the brown cloth surrounding it and the red candle flickering in front of it, I decided to linger rather than to eat with the others.

The longer I lingered, the more I felt drawn into a deep-down stillness as, in my imagination, I pictured Jesus dangling from that cross. The recollection of his agony drew from me a deep, spontaneous and silent adoration. While I was still gazing, contemplating and adoring him, I seemed to see him turn to me as, on that Good Friday, he had turned to John and Mary. Love was streaming from his face. Love flowed from his hands, his side and his heart. It swirled around me and into me. Then, a root seemed gently to push its way out of the tree and wrap itself around me in a protective way so that I found myself in a hidden, underground womb-like space and, although I remained quite still, I knew that, should I want to move, I would simply be responding to the music of liquid love. I could do nothing but stay there and savour the experience. After lingering for an hour or so, the inflow of love seemed to touch a deep fissure at the

core of my being so that, somehow, I knew I was being set free
to give love in a richer measure than ever before; that I could
now operate from a heart which is more healed than hurting.
This love flowed first to Jesus. As I put it later that day in a
letter to a friend: 'I wanted to embrace the cross – to hold it to
myself until it became a part of me, until it entered me. I adore
that man on the cross who has re-created me.'

Such prayer experiences are life-changing gifts from God,
tailor-made by God for each individual. As life-changing as my
contemplation of the 'bush' fire I mentioned in Chapter Three.
There I described how the vine terraces surrounding our home
still bear the scorch marks of the flames which recently burned
them. What I did not say in that chapter was that this planned,
routine fire became the victim of a sudden change in the direction
of the wind. This wind fanned the small, controlled fire into a
blaze sending flames leaping up terraced slopes and racing along
vineyards until in a matter of minutes, they reached our garden
hedge. They singed the roses before starting to lick the jasmine
which climbs up a wooden pergola. We were away from home
at the time, so only heard about the drama when we returned.
But as I now gaze out on to vast stretches of blackness, I am
constantly reminded that, but for the bravery of our neighbours
– a young mother and an elderly widow who were quick-witted
enough to seize the hose pipes in the garden and keep the blaze
under control until the fire engine arrived, our home might not
be here. I am reminded, too, how my attitude towards these
two women has changed. To say that I am grateful would be
an understatement. I am aware that I am indebted to them for
life and find myself yearning to repay them in some way.

When we ponder prayer experiences like the Good Friday
one I have described, the effect is similar. They draw us
closer to Jesus. His gifts of love humble us and stir up within
us the gratitude which gives birth to a desire to serve and
to give him ourselves. In turn, this increases our attachment to him. And the good news is that the deeper this
attachment becomes, the faster we grow into the people he
always intended we should be. For true freedom has nothing to do with pleasing oneself. Paradoxically, true freedom

means to be dominated by Jesus; to be under the influence
of Love.

The place where we are set free to let go

By comparing and contrasting Eve's part in the Fall (Genesis
3:1–24) with the Temptations of Jesus (Matthew 4:1–11), I will
attempt to illustrate what I mean.

When Satan sidled up first to Eve and subsequently to Jesus,
two questions begged to be answered. The first was: 'Whose
Kingdom are you serving?' The second: 'What is your life
principle?' A life principle is the motto we apply to specific
choices and circumstances.[9] When Satan drew Eve's attention
to the seeming lusciousness of the forbidden fruit, she enacted
the answers to these questions showing that she was serving
the kingdom of self and that her motto was: 'I will have what I
want no matter what it costs.' Jesus, on the other hand, gazed on
the stones which must have looked so much like pitta bread, yet,
despite his hunger, he enacted his answers to these questions.
In effect he proclaimed: 'I will not be governed by the pleasure
principle, I will be governed by the Word of God because I am
here, not to please myself, but rather to usher in the Kingdom
of God.'

Just as Satan tempted both of them through the eye gate, by
drawing their attention to something which attracted them, so
he tempted both of them to pursue power. Again, this is where
the similarity begins and ends. While Eve's yearning to 'be as
God' caused her to capitulate, Jesus's submission to the Father
prompted his refusal to be piqued into proving his divinity.

Finally, Satan played his trump card by enticing both of them
to avoid taking responsibility for their actions. Again, while Eve
showed her true colours by stepping into Satan's snare and by
later attempting to pass the blame for her misdemeanours on
to Adam, Jesus neatly side-stepped the trap with a protest.
In effect, he was saying: 'I will not try God's patience for the
sake of prestige or popularity. I will take full responsibility for
my choices.'

The net result of these confrontations was that while Eve lost the freedom to become the poised, responsible person God had created her to be, Jesus emerged empowered. Free. The man of stature and authority his Father created him to be. His attachment to God was so strong that nothing could drag him away from the Father's plan or expressed will. On this occasion, even though he had not eaten for forty days, he could hold a stone on the palm of his hand, know that he possessed the ability to turn it into pitta bread and choose, instead, to say to the Father: 'I'm hungry. I would like to eat. But I am prepared to continue my fast if this is better for the Kingdom.' Even more startlingly, in Gethsemane, he could confess that he did not want to be crucified but he could hold even his life-blood on an open palm and say to his Father: 'You choose.'

This is freedom. This is the life-style of the man who shows us how to become the person God created us to be.

If we piece together the insights of some psychologists, it becomes apparent that Satan is still tempting us through the eye gate, that is, through the lure of the attraction we see. Sigmund Freud suggested that the libido or pleasure principle lies at the heart of every human problem. Alfred Adler questioned this surmise, offering the counter-suggestion that 'the basic drive in people is for power and accomplishment.'[10] The determinist B.F. Skinner contends, however, that we are conditioned by our past and have no alternative other than to abdicate all responsibility for our lives. Who we are and what we become has been decided for us by our up-bringing.

We need not concern ourselves here with a debate about which of these three men is right and which is wrong. We need, rather, to draw on the collective wisdom of all three to recognise that, deep down, all of us have a pleasure-seeking streak, all of us are power-thirsty and all of us are bent towards pride and self-pleasing. We therefore struggle with any principle encouraging us to ensure that it is always God's Kingdom we promote and not our own. If we would be like Jesus, intimacy with God is therefore a must.

Deepening our relationship with God

All friends discover their own methods of becoming more and more intimate with one another. The same is true of closeness with God. And many books are now available to help us in this quest. The book which I have used almost daily for the past nineteen years is Jim Borst's *Coming to God*.[11] In it, he explains that the prayer of relationship or contemplative prayer, as he calls it, sets us free to become the people God intended us to be:

> In the presence of God, we learn the necessity of being absolutely true to ourselves and absolutely honest with ourselves. We learn to see ourselves as we really are – behind the mask of convention and deception, pose and pretence. We grow into truthfulness and genuineness as we grow out of artificiality and falseness in thought, word and deed. The more we live in the presence of God, the more truly we become ourselves – the people God always intended us to be. And as we become more true to ourselves, we become more true to God.[12]

He goes on to claim, and I agree with him, that contemplative prayer also transforms us:

'True spirituality and true prayer must change us, otherwise they are irrelevant and scandalous. We cannot pray day after day, month after month and remain the same.'[13]

One reason why I have used his book so consistently for so many years is that it is a book to be prayed with, rather than a book to be read. Another is that the author takes us by the hand, as it were, and leads us, step by step, out of the fast lane and into a layby with God. There is not space here to do justice to the twelve stages of prayer he mentions in the book – just enough space to whet the appetites of those who sense that they are being drawn into a deeper relationship with God.

The phase of relaxation

The first step is to remind ourselves of Jesus's invitation to 'come . . . and *rest*'. We therefore pull out of life's fast lane for a while, find a suitable layby, take our foot off the accelerator of our heart and relax. It helps, if at all possible, to find a layby into which we can retreat daily: a spare room in our home, a favourite chair in a quiet room, an empty church, a shed in the garden cleaned out specially for the purpose. When we cross the threshold of this place of prayer, it is rather like entering the home of a friend – the opportunity to change gear and to prepare ourselves to deepen the friendship.

Then, just as we might call out our friend's name as we were opening their door, so it can help as we begin our prayer, simply to whisper the name Jesus or to pray: 'Come Holy Spirit', as though we were inviting our indwelling God to come to meet us. Apart from this, during the first few minutes of the prayer time, we say nothing. Instead, just as we might hug a friend on arrival, savouring the richness of the love of this particular relationship, so we spend several minutes tuning in to the presence and love of the Divine Friend who yearns for this time with us even more than we do.

Two friends meeting in this way might then enjoy sharing their news with each other. In the same way, as we become more still in the presence of the Divine Friend, we become aware of the concerns and joys which are uppermost in our minds, letting them tumble out just as they will: the joys, the plans, the worries, the niggles, the questions. As someone has put it, the only way we can come to God is 'just as we are'. And as another teacher of prayer has described the progression as we approach this type of relationship with God, during this first phase of prayer, we become very conscious that it is 'me and him' in that order.

It is at this stage that our prayer differs from a casual conversation with a human friend. For Jesus desires, not simply to hear about the things which concern us, but to lift the burdens from us, at least temporarily, so that we move into a spacious internal place where we can receive his love afresh. So he invites us to transfer our burdens on to him. I sometimes like to picture Jesus in the room where I am praying. When I sense his out-stretched hands, I enact Peter's advice when he says: 'Let him have all your worries and cares, for he is always thinking about you and watching everything that concerns you' (1 Peter 5:7, LB). In other words, I place into those still-scarred hands everything that would prevent me from drawing close to him and him to me. When I have transferred all the clutter from me to him, I stretch out my empty hands as a sign that the hands of my heart are also up-lifted, empty and open, ready to receive anything and everything he desires to give me.

Occasionally, when the burden in my heart seems too big to hold to him, I sense him come to me, lift it from me himself, show me the huge hole which is left when the burden is removed, and remind me that this inner emptiness is the very place into which he will pour fresh and generous portions of his love.

The responding phase

In other words, the encounter begins as we respond to Jesus's invitation: 'Come with me . . . and rest.'

The encounter continues as a deeper response stirs in our hearts and we find ourselves, not only relaxing in his presence, but surrendering to him afresh. This response is not unlike giving a friend a long, leisurely embrace. Not a bear hug. Not a slap on the back. But the kind of non-erotic embrace where genuine love is expressed as your body touches and yields to your friend's. I find Jim Borst's slow, meditative invitation helps me to yield to God in this way:

Before God's face, aware of his presence,
surrender every aspect of your being
your hands, your wrists, your arms;
your senses and brain;
your feet and legs;
each and every nerve and muscle, blood vessel and organ.
Return yourself to him. Seek to withdraw your possessiveness and beg him to possess you, to live in and through you so that you can say with Paul: 'I no longer live, but Christ lives in me' (Galatians 2:20) . . .
urrender your heart, your feelings, your love . . .

Surrender your whole personality, your feelings and all
that is you . . .[14]

The reflecting phase

Just as, often, when we embrace a friend in this healing way, we
marvel at the depth of their love for us, so we may find ourselves
at this stage of our prayer, marvelling at the immensity of the
love in which we are now enfolded. Jesus, God's only son, is here
present with us, attentive to us. This in itself is truly amazing.
Our name is engraved on the palms of his hands.[15] He loves
us so much that he never takes his eyes off us.[16] He indwells
us and we live in him.[17] His life in us is like sap rising to feed
and renew us. His Spirit prays for us continually. He is praying
for us now.[18] He loves us better than we love ourselves. He
knows us better than we know ourselves. Yet he accepts us
as we are. He is using this prayer to change us. We may not
discern precisely how the transformation process works, but it
is happening in the same way as yeast leavens the lump.

He loves us so much that he took the initiative in instigating
this friendship with us.[19]

We sink deeper and deeper into this awareness, deeper and
deeper into his love, and deeper and deeper into heartfelt
gratitude and praise.

The recollecting phase

Or, as we find ourselves enfolded in divine love, we may find
a wave of unworthiness sweeping over us and crashing in a
foaming froth on the shore of our heart. Perhaps this is to
be expected? It so often happens, I find, that when someone
expresses love for me, because I know myself so well, I
know that there is a sense in which I am unworthy of their
affection.

In our relationship with God, we need to refrain from brushing
these feelings to one side and to examine them instead. They
conceal insights which will help us to discover the kind of person
God intended us to be.

So we beg the Holy Spirit to shine the torch-light of his love into the nooks and crannies of our hearts and to expose anything which lurks there which might hinder our relationship with him or which might prevent us from becoming the person God created us to be.

Again, I find Jim Borst's explanation and instructions helpful:

Many of our 'natural' reactions are expressions and gestures of non-acceptance, of rebellion, of running away from reality, of suppression. Anger flares up, impatience possesses us like an evil spirit; dislikes and grudges harden our hearts; we resent interference and interruption. Without always realising it, we often refuse to accept people, events, situations, conditions, even ourselves as God wills them for us and as he accepts them for us. This non-acceptance of his will in concrete circumstances is experienced in prayer as a barrier, a road-block on the way to God. It is his will that we accept people, circumstances, events; that we do not try to influence people or events except by the power of love, forgiveness, suffering, acceptance and thanksgiving. In daily life, this means that we seek to avoid being judgemental, argumentative, critical and interfering in matters that do not concern us.

Ask God to make you aware of actual barriers of non-acceptance in your life . . .

Lay down your will and try to discern God's will . . .

Forgive from the heart . . .[20]

The repenting phase

By this time, unworthiness may be accompanied by conviction or even guilt. But this is not a time or place to grovel. Rather it is an opportunity to confront reality. We are sinful; soiled in so many ways: in our bodies, minds and spirits. We talk to God about our failures and handicaps, lay our sin at the foot of his Cross and stretch out to him stained hands as we beg for pardon. And we give him the privilege and joy of cleansing and renewing us. We may even ask him to show us precisely what it is that he is doing for us.

I remember doing this while praying with a friend on one occasion. She had been pouring into my lap an account of the way in which she had found herself rebelling against God and consequently wounding his love. She now wanted to come back to him in penitence and faith.

As we prayed together over this failure and asked God to cleanse and renew her, a sequence of pictures played on the screen of my mind, showing me, I sensed, the nature of the miracle God was performing at that moment.

In the first picture, I saw a pair of bronzed hands and felt drawn to the long, sensitive fingers. In the second picture, the hands were holding a white, creased piece of fabric which looked like linen. In the third picture, the fingers were shaking out the creases and exposing a large stain which was spoiling the fabric. I then saw that near the hands stood a trough filled with water. As I continued to watch, the hands plunged the cloth into the water, held it there for several minutes and then pulled it out and held it up. The stain had disappeared and the fabric looked new. When I described the pictures for my friend, she expressed her own interpretation – her awareness that, in his love, God had held her in the cleansing waters of his love, removed the stain and renewed her.

He will do the same for us over and over again. That is why, with confidence, we can abandon sin, guilt and discouragement to his immense, unending love, turn away from it and walk away to enjoy the freedom to be the person he made us to be – free in Christ.

The receiving phase

We started this prayer, as I explained earlier, more conscious of ourselves than of God. As the prayer progresses, the emphasis gradually changes until self slips into the wings and we bring Jesus centre-stage. Now the focus changes again. We continue to give Jesus his rightful centre-stage space, but, once again, we draw near.

We concentrate on him, watch him, gaze at him, listen to him. As someone has expressed the purpose of this phase, we look at him because we love him, we look in order to have our love for him rekindled and we look until our love is fed and deepened by our gaze.

And we watch what happens. God responds. He turns to us. Speaks to us. Fills us afresh with his Spirit. We receive all that he offers: joy, guidance, encouragement, peace, insight . . . We bask in the assurance of his love. We submit all that we know of ourselves to all that we know of him: the Truth. His presence provides a new perspective. He, the source of truth, draws us deeper into the truth – the truth about ourselves, the truth about himself and the strength to move back into the fast lane to be more true to both; more capable of giving expression to our authentic selves.

For personal reflection

1. Ask God to deliver you from the curse of superficiality.
2. Re-read p. 48 from 'Aren't you, like me, hoping that some person . . . Once you have touched wet ground you want to dig deeper.' Reflect on it. Make your personal response to it. Write a prayer which is born out of your reflection.
3. Ask yourself the question: 'Whose Kingdom am I serving – the Kingdom of Christ or the kingdom of self?' Then ask another: 'What is my life principle or motto?'
4. Pray the phases of prayer, paying particular attention to the phases of relaxation and receiving.

Notes for Chapter Four

1. Richard Foster, *Prayer* (Hodder and Stoughton, 1992) p. 1.
2. Richard Foster, *Prayer*, p. 1.
3. Richard Foster, *Prayer*, p. 1.
4. Richard Foster, *Prayer*, p. 2.
5. Henri Nouwen, *Life of the Beloved* (Hodder and Stoughton, 1993) p. 26.
6. Henri Nouwen, *Life of the Beloved*, p. 28
7. Henri Nouwen, *Life of the Beloved*, pp. 30–1
8. Henri Nouwen, *Life of the Beloved*, p. 37

9. Here I am drawing on the insights of John Powell in his book *Unconditional Love* (Argus Communications, 1978) ch. 1.
10. Alfred Adler, quoted by John Powell S.J. in *Unconditional Love*, p. 21.
11. Jim Borst, *Coming to God* (Eagle, 1992).
12. Jim Borst, *Coming to God*, p. 57.
13. Jim Borst, *Coming to God*, p. 54.
14. Jim Borst, *Coming to God*, p. 28.
15. Isaiah 49:16.
16. Psalms 139:3.
17. John 17:2–23.
18. Hebrews 7:25.
19. 1 John 4:19.
20. Jim Borst, *Coming to God*, p. 24.

5

SET FREE BY THE TRUTH

The truth is liberating. If we can find it, we discover the secret for which we are searching: who it is we were created to be. And Jesus reveals where this secret may be found:

'If you make my word your home . . . you will learn the truth and the truth will make you free' (John 8:31–2 JB).

In other words, truth needs to be acquired and grasped and learned.

In Hebrew thought, the truth was that which holds water; that which does not give way or collapse; that which is real, correct, a sound basis for conduct. The Bible speaks of a three-pronged truth: the truth is revelation in the form of a person, Jesus; the truth is revelation in the form of a 'letter from home', the Bible; and the truth is God's Word applied to our individual situation by the enlightnenment of God's agent of truth, his Holy Spirit, so that God's truth becomes enfleshed.

'The word', on the other hand, is used to refer both to the written Word, the Bible and the incarnate Word, Jesus himself. As to the concept of setting up home in the Word, Psalm 119 introduces us to a man who seems to have done just that. Here we find the Psalmist striding purposefully in the Law which he respects with his whole being. He brings his entire concentration to bear on each of the commands of the God for whom his heart longs. He thinks constantly about the Word, storing it in his heart (v. 10), treasuring it (v. 11), reciting it (v. 13), meditating on it (v. 15) and delighting in it. The roots of longing burrow deep into his innermost being as he feasts on God's law (v. 20).

He senses that this active Word possesses the power to change him and this gives birth to a holy impatience: 'Wasting no time, I hurry to observe your commandments' (v. 60, JB). It also gives rise to a cry from the heart: 'Lord, don't let me make a mess of things!' (v. 13, LB). 'I am but a pilgrim here on earth: how I need a map – and your commands are my chart and guide' (v. 19, LB).

A growing number of Christians, it seems, are detecting within themselves an envy of the Psalmist. Like beggars holding out the bowl of their spiritual poverty, they clamour to be led to the banquet which they sense has been spread for them in the pages of the Bible. Tired of existing on crumbs, they hanker for the meat and wine of the Word. When someone shows them how, they delight to make their home in God's Word just as the Psalmist did. They discover, with awe, that the many layers of their being, body, mind and spirit, can be nourished, informed and set free by God's liberating Word.

Set free by Bible Study

When we find ourselves among those who are hungry for the Word of God, we need to remind ourselves that, if the Word is going to change us as well as challenge and inform us, we need the anointing of God's Spirit. Andrew Murray put this persuasively one hundred years ago:

> The Word will not take root in us unless the indwelling Holy Spirit quickens us – causing us to accept and appropriate it in the inner life. The Word is a seed. In every seed there is a fleshy part, in which the life is hidden. One may have the most precious and perfect seed in its bodily substance, and yet, unless it be exposed in suitable soil to the influence of sun and moisture, the life may never grow up. And so we may hold the words and the doctrines of Scripture most intelligently and earnestly and yet know little of their life and power. We need to remind ourselves and the Church unceasingly, that the Scriptures which were spoken by holy men of old as they were moved by the Holy Spirit,

can only be understood as they are taught by the same Spirit. 'The words I have spoken are Spirit and Life; for the apprehending and partaking of them, the flesh profiteth nothing: it is the Spirit that quickeneth, the Spirit of Life within us' (John 6:63).[1]

He goes on to underline that this is one of the solemn lessons which the history of the Jews in the time of Christ teaches us. They were zealous, as they thought, for God's Word and honour and yet events were to reveal that all their zeal was for their human interpretation of God's Word. So Jesus had to rebuke them: 'You diligently study the Scriptures because you think that by them you possess eternal life. These are the Scriptures that testify about me, yet you refuse to come to me to have life' (John 5:39).

They did indeed believe that the Scriptures would lead them to eternal life, yet they failed to see that Jesus was the fulfilment of the Old Testament prophecies and so they refused to come to their Messiah. They studied and accepted Scripture in the light and pride of their human understanding rather than in the light and power of God's illuminating Spirit.

Tragically, the same thing can and does happen to believers today. They study the Bible. They know chunks of it by heart. But it has not touched their will or their emotions because they have not looked to the life-giving Spirit to enlighten them. Andrew Murray concludes:

What is needed is very simple: the determined refusal to attempt to deal with the written Word without the quickening Spirit. Let us never take Scripture into our hand, or mind, or mouth, without realizing the need and the promise of the Spirit. First, in a quiet act of worship within you; then in a quiet act of faith, yield yourself to the power that dwells in you and wait on Him, that not the mind alone, but the life in you, may be opened to receive the Word.[2]

There is no one way of steeping ourselves in the Bible under the guidance of the Holy Spirit but a whole variety of ways. Different personalities, at different stages of their spiritual growth will find different methods helpful.

One option is Bible Study.

In my early years as a Christian, my mentors insisted that I should study the Bible, so I spent hours poring over Scripture with the aid of a pile of Bible commentaries. I found it fascinating. That is why I read Theology at university and even attempted to learn New Testament Greek to help me in my quest to understand the text before me. My mind was enriched by these spiritual gymnastics. More importantly, I discovered that studying the Scripture gave me a glimpse of the kind of person God had created me to be.

Take the Bible's teaching on the person and work of the Holy Spirit, for example, which I outlined in Chapter Three. As I traced the Bible's teaching on these subjects, my mind and heart became like that fertilised soil Andrew Murray mentions. My heart was being prepared to receive the seed-bearing Spirit in a new way so that I found myself begging for the privilege of giving birth to his fruit.

This discovery enabled me to take a stride forward in identifying the me God made me to be because, as I have explained in Chapter Three, it is the Holy Spirit whose ministry it is to transform us until we do become a new creation – the person we were always created to be.

Finding a suitable method

In addition to taking a particular subject like the person and work of the Holy Spirit, noting and looking up all the references on the subject mentioned in the concordance, there are a number of other methods of Bible Study.

One is to read the Bible straight through from Genesis to Revelation just to gain an over-view, among other things, of the kind of people God created us to be. Another is to read the Bible right through, underlining every command we discover or placing a mark against all the promises with which the pages of the Bible are peppered.

Yet another is to learn to pray the Psalms, taking note of the way the Psalmist expressed the full gamut of human emotions and learning to emulate him.

But that is not all. When studying the parables, for example, a great deal can be gleaned about God's plan for us if we ask ourselves some probing questions:

'What is the culture in which Jesus spoke?'

'Who is Jesus's audience on any given occasion: disciples, Pharisees or the crowd? What are they thinking?'

'Is Jesus defending the Gospel or instructing the faithful?'

'How would the listeners have interpreted the metaphor or story?'

When we respond intelligently and in an informed way to these and allied questions, the punch-line of the story becomes obvious, revealing to us the kind of people God created us to be.

Take Jesus's parable of the funeral, for example. The time of Jesus's Crucifixion was fast approaching and he 'resolutely set out for Jerusalem' (Luke 9:51). As he walked along the road, he said to a particular individual: 'Follow me.'

'But the man replied, "Lord, first let me go and bury my father." Jesus said to him, "Let the dead bury their own dead, but you go and proclaim the Kingdom of God"' (9:59. 60)

As Professor Kenneth Bailey reminds us, Jesus's listeners would have known that in Middle Eastern culture, a son was expected to stay at home and serve his parents until they died. Then he was free to leave. So they would have understood the man's response to mean, in effect: 'Let me go and serve my father while he is alive and after he dies I will bury him and commit my life to you.'[4] In other words, the man was in bondage to his culture and therefore not free to follow Jesus. Whereupon Jesus throws down the gauntlet by making it clear that what he expects of us is that we become believers who are prepared to swim against the cultural tide. This is part of the cost of being a disciple. He goes on to say that the spiritually dead can take care of the traditional responsibilities of the local community.

Through studying a parable like this, we are given a clear idea of ways in which we can deal with our culture. This is important because one of the biggest barriers to becoming the person God created us to be is worldliness. 'The world,' according to Michael Green, 'means society which leaves God out of account.'[5] If we accept this definition, worldliness implies the subtle infiltration into our innermost beings by society's philosophies, values and attitudes. The pull of the peer group or the boardroom, the team or the gang, is very strong. So is the tug of the media. So a research student may find himself using the department's photocopier without recording what he owes: 'Everybody does.' The young professional might arrive late for work or leave early and think nothing of it: 'Everybody does.' A sixth-former might remove stationery from school for personal or Sunday School purposes: 'Everybody does.' Tax-payers might find illegitimate ways of avoiding the tax-man's demands: 'Everybody does.' A church fellowship might infringe the copyright of books or cassettes, videos or compact discs: 'Everybody does.' And we remain blissfully unaware that these practices are blocking our pathway to freedom and preventing us from becoming the person God created us to be.

More subtly and perhaps more seriously, the cultural norm has bewitched us. It persuades us that the secret of our identity is to be found in the size of our pay packet or in the geographical area where we live or in the place where we spend our holidays. So we climb the professional ladder, trampling on others if necessary, in order to reach the top so that we can earn yet more money. Prestige and possessions, popularity and power, become the gods we secretly worship. And we remain blinded to the reality that unless these are held on an open palm, they will strangle our God-given personality, refusing us permission to be the humble, generous, care-free, compassionate people God created us to be.

More methods of Bible Study

Another way in which our Bible Study can aid us in our attempt to discover who we are in Christ and what it is he intends us to be is to work our way through a book of the Bible, asking ourselves another series of questions:

'What does this passage or book really mean?'
'Why did the writer express it in that way?'
'Why did he choose that particular word?'
'What was he intending to convey?'
'What would it have communicated to the original readers?'
'What does it imply for today's Christians?'
'What is God saying to me?'

To enable us to respond accurately to such questions, we shall want, from time to time, to reach for the commentaries, the concordances, the Bible dictionaries and other aids to help us deepen our understanding. This spade work is illuminating. It reveals the meaning of the original Greek or Hebrew words as well as the cultural context: the history and geography of Palestine, the social customs of contemporary and ancient village life, and the teaching style of Middle Eastern theologians.

Yet another way of studying the Scriptures is to attempt to discover what God says about pressing problems or particular pleasures like marriage, sexuality, friendship, giving, service, ambition, handling temptation, euthanasia, suffering, Sunday trading, debt, to mention a few.

I find it helpful, from time to time, to home in on a topic which currently concerns me. I sometimes do this while I am on retreat. I think, for example, of the occasion when my husband and I had gone on retreat, in part, to ask God to shed his light on our future. We had resigned from the leadership of the church we had worked in for nineteen years and had been invited to work for the church overseas. As the retreat wore on, the sense that God was calling us to leave England, at least for a while, became increasingly strong. I longed to be able to say a ready and joyful 'Yes' to the new vocation which was beginning to take shape. Instead, my mind seemed to focus on the sacrifices we would have to make if we responded to this call.

At this time, I found myself using the word 'grace' very frequently while I was writing in my prayer journal so I decided to make a study of this little-understood word. First I looked up all the references to the word in the Old Testament, then I turned to the New. After that, I referred to a Bible dictionary where I was reminded that the word 'grace' means, among other things, the love of God expressed as 'mercy' (used one hundred and forty-nine times in the Old Testament), 'kindness' (used thirty-eight times), loving-kindness (used thirty times), and 'goodness' (used twelve times). It also speaks of faithfulness and undeserved favour.

As the Bible translator Moffatt put it, Christianity 'is a religion of grace . . . no grace, no gospel'. Or, as the dictionary I was reading expressed it: 'every process of the Christian life is due to grace.' We are called by grace (Galatians 1:15); we are justified by grace (Romans 3:24); by the grace of God we are what we are (1 Corinthians 15:10), and by the grace of God we enter into the fullness of salvation (Ephesians 2:8).

As my mind juggled with these and other pieces of the jig-saw, I found a two-word picture taking shape. The words were: 'pure gift'. God's grace is pure gift. Our vocation is a gift, our salvation is a gift, our personality is a gift. I knew that I needed this gift to enable me to say 'Yes' to becoming the person God created me to be. I fell asleep that night begging for the gift. At three in the morning, I woke with that 'Yes' on my lips. It was another of those gloriously liberating moments when I knew that my attachment to Christ had been strengthened and that consequently I had been cut free from the need to cling to all I held dear, free to hold everything on an open palm, free to stretch out open hands knowing that whatever came into those hands next would come to me with the God I love.

The purpose of Bible Study

It is vital that we remember that the one purpose of Bible Study is not to accumulate facts *per se*, helpful to our meditation as these facts are. The purpose of Bible Study is that we may go beyond the written Word to encounter the Living Word, Jesus, to deepen our relationship with him and to be changed into his likeness.

Jesus himself makes this quite clear. Addressing a group of

rabbis and approved teachers of the Law on one occasion, he observed:

'You diligently study the Scriptures because you think that by them you possess eternal life. These are the Scriptures that testify about me, yet you refuse to come to me to have life' (John 5:39).

Those of us who delight in making our home in the Word of God through Bible Study need to heed this observation, just as those who clamour for more teaching in churches need to heed it. As Paul discovered, the study of the text can become a substitute for a living encounter with the Living Word. It can even become a way of avoiding such an encounter. When this happens, our study of the Bible could lead to the kind of living death Paul recalls:

'The letter kills, but the Spirit gives life' (2 Corinthians 3:6).

The letter can kill because it can lead to spiritual pride, what C.S. Lewis called 'priggery'. The spiritual prig pleads, 'Give us more teaching.' But the abundance of Bible knowledge inflates him with the puffed-up pride Jesus so loathed in the Pharisees. The spiritual prig boasts about the number of Bible verses he can recite by rote but pays no attention to Jesus's insistence that we should incarnate the Word – flesh it out in the nitty gritty of our daily lives. The spiritual prig insists that his interpretation of the Biblical text is foolproof, irrefutable, right. The implication is that everyone else is wrong.

The letter can kill because it can convince us that all we need to do to grow in grace is to store more and more information about God in the computer of our brain. But knowledge does not necessarily affect behaviour. I was reminded of this while writing this chapter. Since I was awake in the early hours of the morning, I decided to get up while it was still dark and therefore cool. I sat at my desk, switched on the light and began to write. I know, of course, that, in this part of the world, if you sit in a room with the windows wide open and the lights on, a motley collection of wild-life will join the party. First came the moths – some of them drowning in my cup of coffee. Then came the cicadas leaping from floor to desk and back again. These were followed by translucent green insects whose names I have not

yet learned. My head told me to close the windows. Instead,
I ignored my head-knowledge and continued to allow nature's
menagerie to cramp my style.

It is so easy to do the same with the head-knowledge we
acquire through Bible study.

We can live with the truth, but not in the truth, let alone living
out the truth. There are even times when, like the student
who came to see me on one occasion, we rebel at the clear
implications of Scripture.

This student described his emotional entanglement with a
fellow student and then proceeded to describe in detail their
homosexual experimentations. He was clearly troubled, wanting
to live life God's way but not knowing what that way was. I
invited him to take a look at the Bible's teaching on such sexual
practices and to draw his own conclusions. He did. Next time
he came to see me, he seemed consumed with anger:

'It's so unfair. The church has explained away divorce. Some
heterosexual Christians even manage to disregard the Bible's
teaching on promiscuity. In twenty years' time they will have
changed their views on homosexual behaviour. I'm just unlucky.
Why should I be stuck with the Bible's rigid teaching on the
subject? It makes me really angry with God.'

Those prophetic words were spoken fifteen years ago. And
my student friend was amazingly accurate. Many Christians
have explained away the Bible's teaching on homosexual activity
and a whole range of other topics also: the sanctity of life, the
need for a day of rest, Sunday trading, the place of women in
marriage, the church and the community, to mention a few.

This approach to God, the pride and rebellion which results
in a Christian adjusting his life-style to God's revealed Word,
is not new. Adam did just this in Genesis 3. It crops up
today with monotonous regularity. When we fall into this
trap, we wave goodbye to a God-given opportunity of growing
into the person he always intended us to become. And it
seems inevitable that, from time to time, we will fall into
this trap. But we need never remain ensnared. As we have
seen, God has given us his Holy Spirit whose mission is to
transform us. He is also the One who persuades us that, to

become truly effective, our Bible Study must flow into Bible meditation.

For personal reflection

1. Experiment with some of the methods of Bible Study suggested in this chapter. When you find a method which works for you at the moment, use it regularly for a while before moving on to other methods.
2. Re-read Jesus's conversation with his would-be follower on p. 65. Notice that Luke does not record the outcome of the man's encounter with Jesus. Put yourself in the man's sandals, as it were. Imagine that *you* have had this conversation with Christ. How would you want to complete the conversation? What is is about your culture which might tug you away from following Jesus wholeheartedly?
3. Write a prayer from your heart which springs from this meditation.

Notes for Chapter Five

1. Andrew Murray, *The Spirit of Christ* (Anson D.F. Randolph and Company, New York, 1888) p. 90.
2. Andrew Murray, *The Spirit of Christ*, p. 90.
3. Professor Kenneth Bailey has lived and worked in the Middle East for the past forty years and has written a number of books on the parables as well as committing his teachings to audio and video cassettes. I am indebted to him for helping me to place the parables in their cultural context.
4. Professor Kenneth Bailey's insight.
5. Michael Green, *I Believe in Satan's Downfall* (Hodder and Stoughton, 1981) p. 53.

6

THE VALUE OF BIBLE MEDITATION

Bible meditation is to Bible Study what snorkelling is to swimming: an eye-opener, the stunning discovery of a hidden wonder world, a way of marvelling at mysteries.

This realisation dawned on me as I was preparing to write this chapter. I was in Oman at the time. On my first visit to one of Muscat's beautiful beaches, I simply enjoyed bathing in the silk-warm water. But on my second visit someone lent me their snorkel. It was then that I discovered that I was not swimming alone as I had thought. Rather I was being escorted by all kinds of exotic fish: blue fish, striped fish, transparent fish, angel fish, cuttle fish – even a baby turtle. Swimming will never again be the same for me. I shall always wonder what accompanies me or whether corals of every colour lie concealed on the sea bed.

Just as it is possible to swim all your life and remain totally unaware of the treasures of the sea, so it is possible to study the Bible all your life and remain blissfully unaware that it can flow into the method of musing or reflecting on God's revealed Word which the Psalmist describes when he writes: 'Oh, how I love you law! I meditate on it all day long!' (Psalms 119: 97). When God gives us the grace to meditate, however, we find ourselves enthralled or shocked by liberating truths which had formerly remained hidden – for meditation leads us beyond and beneath the surface of the written Word to encounter the Living Word. And the Divine Lover delights, in turn, to reveal to us not only himself but our own selves, gradually to transform us into his likeness.

In other words, whereas the study of Scripture primarily engages the mind, meditation on Scripture deliberately engages every part of our personality: not only the intellect, but the emotions also; not only the will, but the imagination and the body, the affections and the senses. In Bible meditation, God speaks to the most intimate depths of our hearts and encourages us to internalise and personalise his in-breathed Word. Then, gently and gradually, the Word changes us by promoting our growth and by bringing us to maturity and an ever-increasing measure of internal freedom.

Methods of meditation

Bible meditation has been in vogue for centuries. As we observed in the last chapter, the Psalmist meditated on Scripture. So did the prophets, Jesus's mother and Jesus himself. Bible meditation was also recognised by the early church. Bishops and teachers of the first seven centuries make this quite clear. They not only absorbed God's Word in their own hearts and minds, they encouraged the faithful to do likewise, drilling them in specific methods.

One ancient method, in particular, seems to be gaining in popularity today. It is the slow, reflective reading of Scripture which Peter Toon calls formative reading. The purpose of formative reading is to be 'formed' by the Word:

that is, to be formed by Jesus Christ through the Holy Spirit, who both inspired and interprets the sacred text . . .
I do not hold the Bible in my hand in order to analyse, dissect or gather information from it. Rather I hold it in order to let my Master penetrate the depths of my being with his Word and thus facilitate inner moral and spiritual transformation. I am there in utter dependence upon our God – who is the Father to whom I pray, the Son through whom I pray, and the Holy Spirit in whom I pray.[1]

So effective Bible meditation begins by coming to God and by pausing until we become aware of his presence. Our body can help or hinder this process. By sitting upright in a straight-backed chair, for example, or by kneeling on a prayer stool and by stretching out our hands in expectancy we can whisper to him and ourselves: 'I'm ready to receive whatever the Holy Spirit wants to give to me or show me today.'

It sometimes happens that, as we pause in this way, the sense of the presence of God fills the room in which we sit. Some people sense this more acutely than others. Whether we feel him or not, we know by faith that he is there loving, listening and speaking because he has promised never to leave us or forsake us.

When we are very tired or have been particularly busy, we may find it difficult to unwind in the way I describe in Chapter Four. At such times, playing quiet music can help us to shed the pressures of the day.[2] One of the quickest ways of shedding these pressures is not to deny them nor to push them on one side but rather to recognise them, name them and then place them, one to one, into the hands of the One of whom Peter wrote: 'Cast your cares on him, knowing that he cares about you' (1 Peter 5:7; my paraphrase).

Reflective reading

Some teachers of prayer liken this period of preparation to laying the table before a meal. When we do it with care, creativity and flair, our attitude to the meal and the people with whom we will share it undergoes a subtle but important change. So it is as we approach the banquet of God's Word.

When we are still and aware of his presence and have reached the stage of receptivity I also highlighted in Chapter Four, we are ready for the feast, so we read the chosen passage of Scripture. When selecting the passage or story for meditation, there is value in choosing one which we have previously studied so that the context and exegesis have been clarified for us. Now, we read it as slowly as possible, refusing ourselves permission to hurry. We read it reflectively, reminding ourselves that, on this occasion, our purpose is not to gather information nor to cover new ground. Rather, we read in order to be nourished, touched, healed and set free by the God who loves us. So as we read, we reverence every word. This means that, just as lovers read one another's letters expectantly and attentively, and just as they discover that a single word or phrase or symbol can speak volumes, so we read expecting our hearts to be touched. We read, not only the words, but between the lines also. We read expecting to be blessed and as one who waits to meet the Living Word who inspired the written Word. We therefore open the hidden parts of ourselves, praying that shafts of God's golden light will penetrate any pockets of darkness lurking inside us. And we become aware that there is a sense in which we are embarking on the same kind of slow, patient, ponderous search archaeologists embark on when they dig. We resolve to continue the search until we find our treasure.

Internalising the Word

This treasure will come to us in the form of a word or a phrase, a verse or a pen-picture which seems, somehow, to peep out from the page. When these words beckon and draw us to themselves, we stop, lay the Bible down and say the word or words over and over to ourselves or we dwell on the pen-picture. We then sink our hearts into the Word, to change the metaphor, in the same way as we sink our teeth into a succulent piece of steak. Gradually we reach the stage of wanting to chew what we have bitten off, in order, first, to extract its full flavour and then to prepare ourselves for the process of swallowing and digesting it.

In other words, this is the stage when we personalise and internalise the Word. There are several ways of doing this. We can ask it questions: 'Is there more to you than meets the eye? What are you saying? What are you saying to me?' We can tell it stories from our recent or past experience. We can receive its blessings, listen to its challenges and pause in case a mental picture rises inside us, allowing us to see or hear or sense the richness of the message.

When we are ready, we receive the Word into our innermost beings, allowing its truth to trickle from our heads into our hearts. We trust that, just as vitamins surreptitiously enrich our bodies when we take them, so the Word is working on us and in us as we assimilate it.

When the words have been sampled and savoured, swallowed and relished, it is time to rest and enjoy the afterglow of the meal. We rest with God, surrendering ourselves to his embrace, luxuriating in the sacredness of the moment

This way, we may find ourselves falling in love with God all over again because, very often, we shall be drinking in the incomprehensible: God is in love with us. As we sense his love flowing into us, we not only trust him, we entrust ourselves to him. We stop searching for him and enjoy the experience of being found by him. We become aware that at the centre of our being lies, not the nothingness or emptiness we feared, but God himself.

Responding and returning

This draws from our heart a response.

Sometimes our response will be laced with awe. Sometimes with gratitude. Sometimes we may find ourselves singing with joy. At other times we may weep the tears of years. Sometimes the Word will leave us protesting or doubting, angry or hurting. Even feeling cheated. At other times it will cause us to gaze at God with deep, heart-felt, passionate, adoring love.

Many people find it helpful to put their hearts on paper by recording their response in a prayer journal. Some write a letter to God expressing their feelings as fully as they can encapsulate them. Others simply jot down key words which would mean nothing to a casual reader but which are pregnant with meaning for themselves and God. Some write poetry. Others make their response pictorially using pastels or paints or felt-tip pens.

Each person will respond in their own way. The method we use is unimportant. What is important is that we allow the Word to make an impact on every layer of our being: our mind and our emotions, our imagination and our will, our attitudes and our relationships, our affections and our desires, our bias to sin and our pain and frustration, our successes and our failures, and the well-spring or core of our entire being. This way we gradually discover how to become the people God intended us to be. This way we will find ourselves tasting the experience James describes when he speaks of look[ing] intently into the perfect law that gives freedom . . . doing it . . . and being blessed in what we do (James 1:25 – see also v. 22).

One of the ways in which this verse is fulfilled in us is that when we have made our response, although we return to our daily routine, we do not stop meditating. The Word which we have digested has become a part of us, so whether we are lying in bed or walking to work, standing in the supermarket queue or caught in nose-to-tail traffic, the Word comes with us. And just as cows chew the cud, so we can regurgitate the Word by bringing it to mind, repeating it and pondering it afresh. This way, new insights may flood into our mind and continue to change our perceptions, attitudes and behaviour in the middle of the muchness and manyness of life. Such is the effectiveness of meditation.

I think, for example, of an occasion when I was extremely tired. I had just arrived home from leading a week-long retreat. Since a relative was in hospital, I had spent two hours with her and then returned home to make a meal for the family. But that evening, as I prepared to meditate on God's Word, I handed to him my tiredness and opened myself afresh to his re-energising Word. Then I read Zephaniah 3:14–20. Verse 17 drew me to itself in rather the same way as a magnet attracts pins: The Lord will renew you by his love (JB).

As I sank my heart[3] into these life-giving words, my mood changed from exhaustion to contentment and as I chewed and digested 'my' verse, I relaxed totally. As I rested with the Word, a mental picture helped me to discern what was happening. I found myself imagining that I was a battery lying in the battery-charger of God's love. There were times when I sensed myself being re-energised by this love so that my mood changed again – from contentment to shalom, that sense of well-being from which flows joy.

In my prayer journal, I recorded the relief I felt that Bible meditation had released me from the down-drag of exhaustion:

Dearest Father,

This prayer time reveals to me afresh how very relevant your Word is to my condition. You know how exhausted I feel today, how my batteries have completely run out of juice. Thank you that . . . you've simply encouraged me to rest and while I've been resting, I know *you've* been re-charging the batteries. Thank you that your arms are the cradle in which I lie and where I can be quietened after a hectic, draining week. Please continue to replenish my resources.

That week seemed full of fresh, daily demands but into each demand I regurgitated my verse: 'The Lord will renew you by his love.' So my attitude changed. Consequently I was set free from frustration, set free to receive the fresh supply of energy which flows from the fingers of God every moment of every day and set free to become the creative person God created me to be.

Other effects of Bible meditation

But it would be dishonest of me to imply that Bible meditation always leaves us feeling nurtured and loved. As I have already hinted, there are times when it appears to leave us desolate. I think, for example, of the first day of one retreat I made when I was meditating in a slightly different way on John 20, verses 19–23 – verses which describe Jesus's appearance to his disciples on the first Easter Sunday evening. While meditating on a Gospel story like this, it can be helpful to picture the scene as vividly as possible and then, rather than simply gazing at the picture as though you are watching a video, to imagine that you are able to step into the picture and interact with the characters concerned.

So, using my imagination, I had stepped into the Upper Room where the disciples had locked themselves into their fear and grief, their shock and bewilderment, and while I was there I had the thrill of encountering the Risen Lord. With the ears of my heart, I had heard his excited greeting: 'Shalom! Peace be with you.' Together with the disciples, I had held my breath as I gazed in adoration at his nail-pierced hands and wounded side. I had sensed the mood change in the disciples as joy percolated through their fear, turning their doubt to trust and faith, and I had taken off the sandals of my heart as Jesus drew near and breathed into me his Holy Spirit. But then, it seemed as though the One who had blessed me so richly and undeservedly suddenly slapped me in the face by saying:

'If you forgive people's sins, they are forgiven; if you do not forgive them, they are not forgiven' (v. 23, GNB).

The love which had welled up in my heart turned to anger and, when I left that Upper Room, I felt cheated and hurt, an emotional wreck.

So I asked myself some pertinent questions. Why did that reference to forgiving others prick the bubble? Could it be that Jesus was putting his finger on something in my life which needed addressing rather urgently? And then the pain of months rushed from the hidden recesses of my heart where I had repressed it.

For months a colleague and I had been locked in conflict. We had worked hard to understand and love one another but all our efforts had failed. It seemed that we had only to be in one another's presence to hurt each other – by a look, a sentence or even a silence. So we had recoiled, stunned and bewildered. Now, it seemed, instead of giving me the reprieve I longed for on this week-long retreat, Jesus was encouraging me to re-open the closed file and do the prayer work without which lasting reconciliation would have been impossible.

That day, my journal recorded not messages of love but rather an out-pouring of pain as I told the Lord how deeply I had felt wounded by this woman. I wrote pages explaining why I felt unable to forgive. In doing this, it was as though an abscess was lanced and the pus of bitterness and hatred burst from me on to the unwitting page of my journal. Even when I had completed this diatribe, I confessed that I still felt unable or unwilling to forgive but I added a tentative request: 'Give me the grace to be willing to be made willing to let go of the hurt and hatred: to forgive.'

Next day, I returned, in my meditation, to the same verse:
'If you forgive people's sins they are forgiven; if you do not
forgive them, they are not forgiven.'

In my imagination, I returned, too, to the Upper Room
where, again, I heard Jesus saying to the disciples and to
me: 'Look at my hands. Look at my side.' This time, I not
only looked, I crept up to Jesus and placed my finger in the
hole in his hand and slipped my hand into the wound in his side.
These wounds reminded me of the brutality of his death – the
price he was prepared to pay so that my many failures might
be forgiven. Slowly, my defences crumbled like chalk. Looking
into my Redeemer's eyes, I was able to pray with integrity the
prayer he taught us to pray: 'Forgive us our sins as we forgive
those who have sinned against us.' I knew that he understood
the full implications of this prayer. I knew, too, that not only had
this Bible meditation set my colleague free from the emotional
corner into which I had pushed her but that I had also been set
free from the poison which had been pulsating around my entire
being, polluting me and many other relationships.

I would have preferred to have begun my retreat on a
much cosier, more comforting note but the purpose of Bible
meditation is not necessarily to bring us comfort, though so
often it does do that. It is to bring us into an encounter with
the God who sometimes deems it necessary to help us clear
away the obstacles which bar us from enjoying the intimacy
he so much wants us to enjoy; who sometimes discerns that
ever-deeper levels of our personality need his healing, liberating
touch so that we can enjoy the wholeness into which he is always
leading us.

Use of the imagination

Some Christians balk at the idea of Bible meditation when
they realise that it involves engaging the imagination. Someone expressed the dilemma in this way when she put the
following in the Question Box during a retreat I was leading:

If I am honest, I do have doubts about the use of the imagination. There are several reasons for this. One is that in Genesis 6:5–6 we read that God was sorry he had made mankind 'for the imagination of his heart was evil continually'. Another is that the tower of Babel surely began in the imagination of man's heart. And in 2 Corinthians 10:5, we read about using spiritual weapons to 'cast down imaginations' (KJV). The imagination, like the rest of us, needs to be redeemed – it *is* being redeemed through the ongoing process of sanctification. But until this work is complete in eternity, do we not need to be cautious with our imagination? Cannot the Evil One who gained access to human imagination in Genesis, all too easily tinker with it today even in the case of a Christian?

If we take comments like these to their logical conclusions, it would appear that we are claiming that whereas at the Fall, Satan gained access to our imaginations, our minds remained gloriously untainted from his malicious meddling. But, of course, that is not true. As a result of the Fall, every part of our personality was affected and can now be used for good or for evil, channelled constructively or destructively. This includes the mind.

As we observed in the last chapter, our mind can convince us of the seeming necessity to live as children of our culture or it can persuade us to challenge our culture by ushering in the counter-culture of God's Kingdom.

Moreover, Paul's reflections on the mind are worthy of note. 'The mind of sinful man is death,' he claims (Romans 8:6). 'The sinful mind is hostile to God. It does not submit to God's law, nor can it do so' (Rom. 8:7). It cannot do so because 'the God of this age has blinded the minds of unbelievers, so that they cannot see the light of the gospel of the glory of Christ, who is the image of God' (2 Corinthians 4:4). Only the mind which is controlled by the Spirit is life and peace (Romans 8:6). We therefore live in constant and urgent need of that ministry Paul calls the renewal of the mind (Romans 12:2).

We also need to note that it is only the Authorised Version

(AV) or King James Version (KJV) which uses the word 'imagination' in the verses from Genesis quoted above. More modern translations seem to recognise that the word 'imagination' in earlier English meant not only the ability to see pictures, but was also shorthand for the thought-patterns of the unregenerate. So, for example, the NIV rendering of Genesis 6:5 reads: 'The Lord saw how great man's wickedness on the earth had become, and that every inclination of the thoughts of his heart was only evil all the time' instead of the older version: 'the imagination of his heart was evil continually'.

But there are other, more positive reasons why we should engage not just our minds but our imaginations also when we meditate on the Bible. The chief reason is that Jesus clearly expected us to do so.

As I underlined in *Open to God*,[4] unlike many of today's scholars and Christian teachers and writers, Jesus was not a Western theologian. He was a Middle Eastern theologian. He did not, therefore, appeal primarily to the intellect. He appealed first and foremost to the imagination, which was why he taught, not through carefully crafted three-point sermons, but through stories which he often left suspended so that his listeners would complete them for themselves. He also appealed to the eye gate, appearing to expect his hearers to visualise what he was describing: the farmer scattering his seed in the way some farmers in the Middle East still sow their crops; the woman sweeping her house with the vigour with which my neighbours here in the Eastern Mediterranean still sweep their homes: the shepherd who, at cost to himself, searched the ditches and dells until he had found and rescued the sheep who was as dear to him as a child. Similarly, Jesus appears to have expected his audience to enter into the parables, using their senses in the way some creatures use their antennae. So he appears to expect us to smell the yeast, to marvel at the effect it has on a lump of lifeless dough, to watch the loaf rising before our eyes.

This causes Richard Foster to conclude, and I agree with him:

We simply must become convinced of the importance of

thinking and experiencing in images. It came so spontaneously to us as children, but for years now we have been
trained to disregard the imagination, even to fear it . . .
The imagination is stronger than conceptual thought and
stronger than the will.[5]

Or, as Gerard Hughes expresses it:

The imagination is a wonderful and much neglected faculty.
It enables us to enter into the scenes of the Gospel with
our senses and our feelings as well as with our minds,
but it also projects into our conscious minds thoughts,
memories and feelings which, although hidden from us in
our subconcious, are, in fact, influencing our perception,
thinking and acting.[6]

Indeed, through using what C.S. Lewis referred to as the
'baptised imagination', our meditation may reveal to us that
our image of God is distorted, that we are riddled with guilt,
paralysed by past pain, crippled by an overwhelming sense of
worthlessness, or full of doubt rather than faith. We therefore
need to discover how to process our meditation so that,
whatever it reveals, we can use it, not to condemn ourselves,
but rather to find a new dimension of freedom.

Processing our meditation

One way of processing our meditation so that it helps us to
discover the kind of people God created us to be is to pause
when we have completed it and ask ourselves some pertinent
questions:
  'What was my predominant mood while I was meditating: joy
or sadness, peace or anxiety, strength or exhaustion, doubt or
hope, fascination or boredom or . . . ?'
  'Or did my moods fluctuate? If so, how? Did I lurch from fear
to faith or . . .'

'Were there times when my mind seemed to go blank or when nothing seemed to be happening? If so, what was happening in the seeming nothingness?'

'Which words or pen-pictures, phrases or experiences seemed particularly helpful?'

'When did negative feelings sweep over me and what name would I give to these feelings?'

'Were there any other obstacles which seemed to block my path to God: guilt, worthlessness, the memory of past hurts, a negative image of God, for example? If so, how have these left me feeling?'

Our response to these questions will determine what happens next. If the meditation left us feeling loved or comforted by God, for example, processing this discovery poses few problems. We can round off our time of prayer by relishing the memories of this fresh encounter with the indwelling Christ, allowing them to re-energise us and equip us for the tasks ahead.

If, on the other hand, our path to God seems blocked for some reason, or if the meditation has left us filled with a feeling of sadness or bogged down with worry, we will need to adopt a different procedure. Take guilt feelings, for example. Guilt can be a healthy reaction to our own wrong-doing. In this event, when guilt surfaces during our meditation, we need only acknowledge our failure and ask for the grace to receive God's free-flowing forgiveness. If we detect an internal struggle, which is not unlike a civil war when one part of our personality longs to repent while the other part remains in a stubborn state of rebellion, it is wise to allow the repentant part of ourselves to pray so that, in time, the other part of us can catch up.

But what about those occasions which happen to most of us from time to time, when guilt overwhelms us with a sense of worthlessness and seems out of all proportion to any misde-meanour we may have committed? What happens when we feel persistently unloved and unlovable? Gerard Hughes speaks helpfully of this not uncommon state of mind when he writes:

Salvador Dali has painted the crucified Christ suspended

above the globe of the earth. Let your imagination work on that image and speak to Christ dying on the cross. He has become the sin of the world and there is no crime, however hideous, which he has not taken on himself and forgiven. Tell Christ that although he has succeeded with the rest of the human race, he has met his match in you, and that not even his death can overcome your guilt. He may find all other human beings to be lovable, but you are God's mistake which he can never put right. If you can persist in this prayer, he will uncover a hidden source of guilt, which is pride, the refusal to let God be God to you, clinging to your guilt as though it were more powerful than his love.[7]

Silence

Gerard Hughes continues:

Another method is to sit in silence with your feelings of guilt and worthlessness, as though they formed a heap of rotting rubbish in front of you, and then pray to Christ to show himself through the mess. This is a useful exercise because in it you are not pretending, not hiding your guilt from yourself; you are acknowledging your own inability to remove it and allowing him to be what we can so easily express with our lips, but not with our inner being – our Saviour.[8]

Our liberator. The One who alone is able to set us free, not only from our guilt and shame but from ourselves also.

And if nothing seems to have happened, we do well to examine the nothingness. Like the man who attended a retreat I was leading on one occasion. I led the group in a meditation on Revelation 3:20 where Jesus says: 'Listen! I stand at the door and knock; if anyone hears my voice and opens the door, I will come into his house and eat with him, and he will eat with me' (GNB).

'Imagine you are in your own home,' I invited the group,

'and you hear a knock at the door. You know it is Jesus, so notice whether you decide to open the door or to pretend there is no one at home. If you open the door, notice whether you do it with a flourish, showing that you are pleased to welcome him or whether you do it reluctantly, aware that the beds are not made or that the washing up has not been done.'

As I continued in this vein, I noticed that this particular man was looking extremely uncomfortable, so during the coffee break which followed, I asked him how he had found the experience.

'It was a complete waste of time,' he retorted angrily.

'Would you like to tell me what happened?' I invited.

'Nothing happened,' he replied curtly. 'I've already told you that it was a complete waste of time.'

'Tell me about the nothing,' I persisted. Whereupon he explained that he lives in a mews flat in London. 'The door of my flat opens outwards,' he went on. 'When you told us Jesus was knocking on the front door, I went to it and opened it with such a flourish that I knocked Jesus over and had to help him to his feet again. That just shows you how stupid the experience was.'

Suddenly his anger evaporated, his jaw dropped and he exclaimed: 'Joyce! That's the story of my life. I've been so busy making money that I've had no time for Jesus recently. It's as though I've been knocking him over whenever he has attempted to come near to me. I see now that it's time to help him to his feet and invite him back into my life again.'

I was touched by the humility of this confession and moved to discover once more that, through Bible meditation, God had begun to put this man back in touch with the person he was created to be.

Such experiences are not rare. Such stories are numerous. The genius of Bible meditation is that it has the capacity to touch the many layers of our personality so that, little by little and bit by bit, more and more parts of our being are set free by God's liberating Spirit.

For personal reflection

1. Re-read the pages on reflective reading and internalising the Word (pp. 75–7). Then turn to Psalm 139 or a passage of Scripture you have been studying recently, and meditate on it in the way I describe. Try too make sure that you leave time to make your response.

2. Read John 20:19–23. Picture the scene as vividly as you can. Ask yourself the questions on pp. 84–5:

   'What was my predominant mood while I was meditating: joy or sadness, peace or anxiety, strength or exhaustion, doubt or hope, fascination or boredom or . . . ?

   'Or did my moods fluctuate? If so, how? Did I lurch from fear to faith or . . . ?

   'Were there times when my mind seemed to go blank or when nothing seemed to be happening? If so, what was happening in the seeming nothingness?'

   'Which words or pen-pictures, phrases or experiences seemed particularly helpful?'

   'Did negative feelings sweep over me at any time? If so, what name would I give to these feelings?'

   'Did anything obstruct my path to God: guilt, worthlessness, the memory of past hurts, a negative image of God, for example? If so, how have these left me feeling?'

   Make your response, bearing in mind p. 85.

3. There are two cassettes which can help people explore the methods of Bible meditation mentioned in this chapter: *Teach Us to Pray* published by Hodder and Stoughton, and *Teach Me to Pray*, published by Eagle. Both include music to bring listeners into stillness and guided meditations.

Notes for Chapter Six

1. Peter Toon, *Meditating as a Christian*, (HarperCollins, 1991) p. 58.

2. Several cassettes have been produced to help people come into this kind of stillness. Among them are: *Open to God* by Joyce Huggett, published by Hodder and Stoughton; *Reaching*

Out, Impressions and *In the Beginning* by John Gerightey and
Simeon Wood, published by Eagle. And many people find music
from the Taizé community, particularly the cassette, *Laudate*, is
especially helpful.

3. Here I am drawing on the insights of Macrina Wiederkehr in her
   book, *A Tree Full of Angels* (Harper and Row, 1988) pp. 49–63.
4. Joyce Huggett, *Open to God* (Hodder and Stoughton, 1989)
   pp. 53–6.
5. Richard Foster, *Celebration of Discipline* (Hodder and Stoughton,
   1980) p. 22.
6. Gerard Hughes SJ, *God of Surprises* (Darton, Longman and Todd,
   1986) p. 37.
7. Gerard Hughes SJ, *God of Surprises*, pp. 84–5.
8. Gerard Hughes SJ, *God of Surprises*, p. 85.

7

HINDERED BY HURTS

Over and over again the Holy Spirit uses the medium of Bible meditation to remind us that we were created for love: both to give love and to receive it. One reason why he does this is to impress on us that we were created in the image of God – that is, in the image of the Holy Trinity: the Father, the Son and the Holy Spirit. This means that we were created to be like this tri-une God. A careful survey of the nature of the love which flows between these three persons who are so mysteriously one, helps to put us in touch with our potential.

Love is mutuality

Take Genesis 1, for example, where we eavesdrop on a conversation taking place within the sacred precincts of the heavenly places. 'God said, "Let *us* make man in our own image, in the likeness of ourselves"' (v. 26, JB, my emphasis). The unmistakable and undeniable use of the plural suggests that, as the Father, the Son and the Holy Spirit discussed the creation of the world, they dreamed another dream – of creating people who, like themselves, would be capable of communicating with each other and co-operating with each other – who could become co-creators with God.

Jesus invites us to take a further peep behind the curtains of the heavenly realms. During the Last Supper, while he prepares his disciples for his imminent departure, he reminisces in prayer: 'And now, Father, glorify me in your presence with the glory I had with you before the world began' (John 17:5). John provides us with a thumb-nail sketch of that glory when, in the prologue of his Gospel, he writes:

'Before the world was created, the Word already existed; he was with God, and he was the same as God . . . Through him God made all things; not one thing in all creation was made without him' (John 1:1, 3, GNB).

Many Bible scholars also believe that Proverbs 8:27–31 (JB) refers to Jesus's relationship with his Father before the Holy Spirit shone like the sun over the darkness which was to become the world:

> When he fixed the heavens firm, I was there,
> when he drew a ring on the surface of the deep,
> when he assigned the sea its boundaries . . .
> when he laid down the foundations of the earth,
> I was by his side, a master craftsman,
> delighting him day after day,
> ever at play in his presence,
> at play everywhere in his world.

By putting together these pieces of the jig-saw, it becomes apparent that, before the beginning of creation, a relationship existed between three co-equal persons. This relationship was characterised by co-operation, communication and two-directional love – giving love and reciprocal love. Since we were born in the image of this tri-une God, it follows that we were born capable of and needing relationship. Indeed, the author of Genesis goes on to underline that even in Paradise an intolerable loneliness held the first man in its deathly grip until the opportunity for relationship with a like-minded person was provided. God's profound statement, 'It is not good for the man to be alone,' seems to have been etched on our souls ever since. It is a cry which finds an echo in so many hearts today. Like Andy – a young man who came to see me while I was in the middle of writing this chapter.

'Impoverished. That's a good word to sum me up. That's just how I feel,' he admitted and went on to relate the way in which this realisation had surfaced for him that very evening.

'I was driving home through the country lanes this evening and the sun was low in the sky, just peering through the trees. It was beautiful. And I thought back to last week when I was on a skiing holiday in the mountains. It was magic, you know. As we reached the top of one mountain, you could look ahead and see mile after mile of virgin snow. Not a single foot-mark marred it. It was wonderful. So much beauty. Such good health. I've got a fulfilling job, too – in fact I have to tear myself away from it, I enjoy it so much. Yet some days I wake up and wonder: is this all life is? And inside me there's an emptiness. I'm hollow, an empty shell. The dull ache gnaws away inside me and I wonder if I can live for another forty years carrying the burden of my aloneness.'

My heart went out to this young man who had grown so keenly aware that a person's deepest need is for relationship because, as we talked, he admitted that he had never learned how to forge close friendships and even now, successful though he was in so many ways, he would not know where to begin.

Difficulties in loving

This problem is not unique to Andy. Many of us would confess to loving with a limp which has handicapped us for years, if not all our lives. We stumble in and out of relationships because we lack self-esteem and, as the contemporary author and psychiatrist Jack Dominian so rightly reminds us: 'To be and feel good in being oneself is the key to self-love and self-love is the key to all personal loving.'[1]

Dr Dominian goes on to put his finger on another reason why many of us become emotional cripples, in his shrewd observation that 'so much hinges on the way our constitutional make-up interacted with the way our parents behaved towards us'.[2] I like this emphasis because the assumption is frequently made that we are who we are because of the things that our parents or other significant people in our lives did or neglected to do. That is not strictly correct. Our parents may have given us what is commonly called today, 'good enough parenting',[3] yet the way we received and perceived their love may have caused us to emerge from childhood into adulthood feeling insecure or of little worth, lacking in self-esteem or self-confidence, unable to receive either affection or affirmation, feeling unloved and unlovable. We may feel so bad about ourselves that, deep-down, we are convinced that who we are and what we have to offer in relationships is worthless.

Childhood vulnerability

Because we come into the world as helpless babies and because the maturing process takes us through the vulnerability of childhood and adolescence, there are endless opportunities for seemingly irrevocable damage to be done.

Take our arrival into the world, for example. For some babies, this is the first joyous adventure into a new environment where clearly they are wanted, loved and cherished: But for others, birth is not an adventure but a trauma. As author and counsellor Edward Moss reminds us:

> there is a good deal of evidence to suggest that if a baby is unwanted or resented, or if the mother herself is ill or miserable or insecure during the pregnancy or the birth, this can make the process more of an exhausting ordeal, less of a joyful venture.[4]

He goes on to explain that such birth traumas can cast long shadows over the person's future.

But our vulnerability accompanies us beyond babyhood and into childhood. Since these are the phases of our lives where important foundations are laid, like trust, self-acceptance, pride in achieving and pleasure of self-expression, our propensity for being badly hurt accelerates. Because children are resilient, they find coping mechanisms to over-ride emotional knocks and bruises at the time they occur. But the patterns of behaviour they devise are not necessarily healthy, neither does the memory of them die. It lives on, capable of being activated in adulthood, when a person comes under stress or, like Andy, flounders in the attempt to make close relationships. The consequences can then be dire.

In *Habitation of Dragons*, Keith Miller records the tragic tale of Alice – a woman whose inability to forge close friendships in adulthood was traced to the emotional injuries inflicted on her when she was a child:

When I was a tiny little girl, I was put in an orphanage. I was not pretty at all, and no-one wanted me. But I can recall longing to be adopted and loved by a family as far back as I can remember. I thought about it day and night. But everything I did seemed to go wrong. I tried too hard to please everybody who came to look me over, and all I did was drive people away. Then one day the head of the orphanage told me a family was going to come and take me home with them. I was so excited, I jumped up and down and cried. The matron reminded me that I was on trial and that it might not be a permanent arrangement. But I just knew it would be. So I went with this family and started school in their town – a very happy little girl. And life began to open up for me, just a little.

But one day, a few months later, I skipped home from school and ran in the front door of the big old house we lived in. No-one was at home, but there in the middle of the front hall was my battered old suitcase with my little coat thrown over it. As I stood there and looked at that suitcase, it slowly dawned on me what it meant . . . they didn't want me. And I hadn't even suspected . . . That happened to me seven times before I was thirteen years old.[5]

Sadly, this is not an isolated incident. Alice's heart-rending testimony could be echoed by far too many people whose ability to trust has been destroyed by repeated rejections. As Jack Dominian explains:

The absence of a safe physical and emotional attachment primes such a person to regard its surrounding world with suspicion. Instead of security it acquires the fear of being abandoned, unwanted or rejected. This fear becomes gradually a part of its life so that it expects those close to it to act in a similar manner. Such a person expects to be let down, rejected, hurt, attacked or even destroyed by others. They are particularly vulnerable to suspicion about the intentions of others. Such vulnerable people find it hard to establish relationships of trust and both their freedom and integrity of relating are restricted.[6]

But Simon was not rejected by his parents. They loved him so much that they wanted the very best for him. They even made huge personal sacrifices so that Simon could be sent to boarding school. Unfortunately, it had not occurred to them to explain to their son why they believed that this particular plan lay in his best interests. So Simon, a sensitive, creative child, was devastated at the age of eleven to be presented with a *fait accompli*: he was to become a boarder at the nearby school.

'Why?' was the question which burned inside him as he struggled to adjust to life away from home. 'What have I done wrong? Why don't they want me at home?' He dared not voice these questions lest his parents should accuse him of being insolent and, as he thought, love him even less. So he fought back the tears which frequently threatened to betray the river of sorrow continually flowing inside him.

He tried to come to terms with the hurly-burly of boarding school which so many of his peers seemed to relish. But he was not the sporty type who quickly gathered round himself a group of like-minded, out-going friends. He was a bookworm who sought privacy and peace where he could indulge in the fascinating world of ideas.

Term after term saw no improvement in his ability to adjust to boarding-school life. At the beginning of every holiday, he determined to pluck up courage to ask his parents if he could become a day boy. Each holiday his courage failed. Gradually, as the years wore on, his ability to give and receive love dwindled to a puddle. But the lovelessness hurt. The hurt gave rise to hatred and anger. No one suspected the inner ferment because Simon succeeded in camouflaging the real situation with a plastic smile.

Simon's story, too, will resonate with many readers – not necessarily because they were packed off to a boarding school against their will or better judgment, but because they have been caught up in other transitions for which they were unprepared.

As Edward Moss reminds us, if these transitions are abrupt:

> there may well be a tendency to create a sort of shell round the inner personality. This shell becomes the outward personality of the child, while the inner, more sensitive side finds no expression, is not encouraged or developed, and gradually disappears from consciousness. This can produce in later years an adult who is rigid in conforming to an image, rather than spontaneous in expressing his or her true self, one who finds it hard to be in touch with his or her emotions, one who is afraid of losing control and whose emotional life is in some degree underdeveloped and immature.[7]

Adulthood

Unfortunately, the human psyche remains vulnerable beyond childhood and into adulthood. Human beings are capable of being emotionally wounded to the day they die.

I recall, for example, a conversation I once had with an elderly member of the church I once attended. When she worshipped, this woman's face would glow with wonder, love and praise, and I loved to watch her. But sometimes, when she and I spent quality time together, she would show me the hurting side of herself. Her husband had died, her daughter had committed suicide and, one by one, the friends with whom she had spent so much of her life had 'died off', as she put it. This left, not only the inevitable ache of bereavement, but a reluctance to reach out to others in love. 'It hurts so much when someone you love is taken away,' she explained.

I understood. We do not need to wait until we are in the upper eighties to experience the sense of loss which sweeps over us when a loved one is removed through death, divorce, or some other separation. We do not need to wait until we are old to discover the reluctance we feel in the wake of such separation to reach out to others and to explore new friendships.

Young adults may find their ability to love blocked for different reasons. I think, for example, of a young man I met on one of my trips to the Far East. We will call him Gee Ming.

Gee Ming used to lead the youth group of the church he attended. He loved the young people and they responded positively and warmly to his leadership. But Gee Ming, a new convert, was a young man with heavy financial commitments. Over a period of time, unknown to anyone in the church, he got into serious debt. Shame about his predicament prevented him from discussing the situation with his pastor or with the elders of the church. Instead, he fell back into a way of coping which had been all too familiar to him before he committed his life to Christ: gambling, speculating, embezzlement and even overt theft. He knew that these practices were wrong but a voice inside him would whisper: 'It will only be for short while, then you can live like a Christian again.' This voice sounded so sensible and so wise. But by the time I met him, he had withdrawn from the fellowship, resigned from leadership of the youth group and was actively avoiding any encounter with his former Christian friends.

'It's over now – the church, I mean. They were my family. It's left a big hole in my life and I don't know how to fill it.'

Gee Ming had become a lonely, lost and forlorn man whose life, at that moment, seemed to be devoid of love.

Again, such incidents are not rare in the experience of young adults. They venture into the big, uncharted sea of work with no one to guide them. Having little or no experience to draw on, they rely on the few insights and strengths they have acquired during their teenage years. When they are brought face to face with situations which challenge their youthful idealism, their limited expertise and even their faith – relationship problems, problems with management, work problems, financial problems, the inability to find employment and so on, their ability to give and receive love may well suffer a severe set-back. Even so, what they urgently need at this time is a great deal of understanding and tender loving care.

If someone like Alice so much as sniffs rejection, she may well curl up in a prickly ball like a hedgehog and become uncommunicative. Or, someone like Simon may well appear to be charming – or sweet if they are a woman – but this charm and sweetness may well camouflage a seething volcano. Unexpected change like redundancy, divorce, adultery, betrayal of other kinds, could cause the volcano to erupt.

Some solutions

That is the bad news. It is bad news because it restricts our freedom to become the loving and lovable people God created us to be. The good news is that we need not live for ever out of an 'unhealed centre'. Healing is available. Very occasionally this healing is instant. Almost always it is gradual. It comes in a vast variety of ways. In this chapter, we high-light two of these ways and in the next chapter home in on many more.

One way is through pastoral counselling or even through psychotherapy. I like the way Edward Moss defines this instrument of healing:

'It is the function of counselling or psychotherapy to provide the framework of concerned attention, love and support, within which the individual is enabled to complete this bit of growing up.'[8]

In other words, a counsellor or psychotherapist may help the person being counselled to trace the problem back to its source and will seek to help them to establish new patterns of behaviour so that they can be set free to become the loving, lovable people God created them to be.

While I was in the middle of writing this chapter, the telephone rang. The caller was a friend who has been on the receiving end of professional counselling for the past two years. 'Outwardly nothing has changed,' she confessed. 'But inwardly, a lot is happening. I know that I am being set free. I know that I am becoming more "me". There's a long way to go yet but I'm getting there.'

Many of us who have benefited from the wisdom, insights and love of sensitive, professional counsellors would echo that confident cry. Like Simon, the young man whose ability to love was impaired by his reaction to his parents' decision to send him to boarding school. He received counselling over a period of many months. During the sessions, he was brought face to face with the questions he longed to put to his parents at the age of eleven. He was able, too, to process the anger which had blazed inside him throughout his childhood and early adult years. He was also able to confront the methods he had used to cope with the problems he encountered at boarding school, face the lessons the experience had taught him about himself and discover how he could re-negotiate life on a new set of terms. Slowly, his latent, God-given ability to love re-emerged.

Simon once likened the healing process to the drip-by-drip thaw which happens when snow and icicles begin to respond to the warmth of rising temperatures. At first he found the melting process alarming. But when he realised that the thaw could be slow and steady, persistent and gentle, his plastic smile was replaced with a genuine one. Little by little he found within himself the resources to reach out a rescuing hand to others in need and, eventually, to learn to ask others for help. He was even able to understand why his parents had acted in the way they did and to let go of the resentment he had harboured against them from puberty on.

Inner Healing

There used to be a time when it was believed that professional counselling was the only route towards wholeness that a person could take. But the past twenty years or so have produced enough evidence to show that God is using other ways to set people free to love and be loved.

I think, for example, of the ministry of inner healing.

Francis MacNutt, a man who has been used by God in the

healing ministry for the past thirty years or so, defines inner healing in this way:

> The basic idea of inner healing is simply this: that Jesus, who is the same yesterday, today, and forever, can take the memories of our past and:
> 1. Heal them from the wounds that still remain and affect our present life.
> 2. Fill with his love all these places in us that have been empty for so long.
>
> The idea behind inner healing is simply that we can ask Jesus Christ to walk back to the time we were hurt and to free us from the effects of that wound in the present. This involves two things then:
> 1. *Bringing to light* the things that have hurt us. Usually this is best done with another person; even the talking out of the problem is in itself a healing process.
> 2. *Praying the Lord to heal the binding effects of the hurtful incidents of the past*.
>
> Some of these hurts go way back into the past; others are quite recent.[9]

As I have explained in *Listening to Others*,[10] I have benefited enormously from this gentle, sensitive ministry. So did Gill.

Gill once worshipped in the same church as me. By her own confession, she was an inquisitive little girl. Like many chidren, she frequently tuned in to adult conversations and, like many children, was quick to absorb facts but slow to interpret them accurately. Since she was a sensitive child, snippets of conversations she overheard would tumble round in her mind as clothes tumble round in a washing machine. Some of the things she overheard seriously dented her self-esteem. When she came to see me on one occasion she vividly recalled and described one such incident.

She was six years old at the time and had gone, with her mother, to the family doctor who was also a friend of the family. After the doctor had given her a routine medical examination,

Gill dressed herself behind the curtained screen where she was out of sight but not out of ear-shot. So she heard the doctor say in a casual, jocular kind of way: 'Of course, you realise that Gill will never be a teacher or anything like that? She's not clever enough.'

This observation not only tumbled round her head, it wormed its way into her heart and lodged there – hidden but neither lifeless nor powerless. Although Gill never consciously recalled the incident as she grew up, from that moment she lived within its limitations.

Throughout her late teens, for example, and even into her early twenties, whenever she was invited to accept responsibility at work or in the church, she would giggle nervously and brush such invitations aside with a dismissive comment like, 'Oh! Thank you ever so much for inviting me but I couldn't do anything like that – I'm not good enough.' It was as though her memory played on her perception of herself the kind of tricks a hall of mirrors plays on peoples' bodies. The reflection she saw was grossly misshapen.

This reflection was unexpectedly exposed when I invited her to become a Sunday School teacher. She refused. But some time later she reopened the conversation:

'You know, I don't understand myself. I really love children, as you know. I think they're really lovely. But when you asked me to be a Sunday School teacher recently, I panicked. "I couldn't. Oh! I couldn't," I said to myself. "Think of all the responsibility. I'm not capable of coping with that. Not good enough." But there's another part of me that knows I *could* do it. And that makes me really cross with myself. I really want Jesus to set me free from whatever it is that's holding me back so that I can serve him as I want to.

When we prayed together, asking God to expose the source of her feelings of inferiority, the old memory of the doctor's surgery flooded into Gill's mind.

I invited her to return, in prayerful imagination, to that surgery; to become, as far as she was able, in her imagination, little six-year-old Gill. She did.

'Yes. I'm there. I can see it all clearly. And I can hear the doctor telling my mother that I wouldn't be clever enough to be a teacher.'

We then went on to ask God to reveal to us whatever he wanted to show Gill about herself.

In the silence which followed, some words from Isaiah came into my mind. Although these words were originally a message for the nation of Israel, they convey comfort for every child of God and I sensed that God was wanting to remind Gill of them now:

> Fear not, for I have redeemed you . . .
> you are precious and honoured in my sight
> and . . . I love you.
>
> (Isaiah 43:1, 4)

> You will be like a beautiful crown for the LORD.
> No longer will you be called 'Forsaken,' . . .
> Your new name will be 'God Is Pleased with Her' . . .
> Because the LORD is pleased with you.
>
> (Isaiah 62:3–4, GNB)

As I read these promises aloud, I heard Gill gasp. She told me what had been happening to her in the silence. In her mind's eye she had seen a picture of a huge hand which she took to be the hand of God. On the open palm, held up for all to see, lay a priceless jewel which God seemed to assure her was the way he viewed her. We had asked him to show us what his perception of Gill was and, with awe, we sensed that he had spoken: through the prophet and through a picture.

It was a liberating moment in that it was as though the finger of God had lifted the arm of the record player from the disc which used to pound out the message: 'You're not clever Gill . . .,' then taken the old record and smashed it. Instead, he sang a new song which was to tumble round Gill's head for a very long time:

> You are precious . . .
>   and honoured . . .

I love you
And I'm pleased with you.

Although the past was still the past, although what had happened in that surgery all those years ago could not be reversed, the sting had now been removed from Gill's memory so that, gradually, it lost its power to restrict her freedom.

I would like to emphasise that word 'gradually'. It is rare that a single prayer reverses the message that the unhealed areas of our lives pump into our consciousness. Inner healing is almost always a process. It was for Gill. Over the months, as she assimilated the new song which now carolled through her brain, she gained in self-confidence and blossomed. She did become a Sunday School teacher and loved it so much that she went on to train as a primary school teacher. While she was training, she also became the worship leader of the church she attended. Some two years after our prayer time together, I talked to her after a meeting. She grinned broadly, brought me up to date with her progress and made the telling comment: 'It's as if I've finally grown up. It's great.'

For personal reflection

1. Read, as slowly and reflectively as possible, Psalm 139:1–18. Just as the Psalmist here reviews his life, take time to review yours. One way of doing this is to write down eight to twelve significant events of your life, beginning with your birth and ending with the present moment. As you recall the past, ask yourself the question:

    'How has God revealed his love to me at various stages of my journey through life?' Relish every memory of his love. Write a prayer of praise and thanks.
2. Or echo this prayer:

    Lord God, we your human children are learning from experience that we must have love; without it we go wrong. We see how little ones without the warm love of father and mother, never really recover. Every soul cries out, 'I want to be loved'. Lord, it takes a lot of faith to think that out of the billions of souls you love each one, as if he were an only child. Nothing can kill your love for me . . . nothing I do, whatever happens to me, wherever I go, even in the hells I make for myself. O Father and Mother God.[11]

3. Reflect on Jeremiah 31:3, (GNB):
    'I have always loved you, so I continue to show you my constant love.'
    And this promise from God:

Your days as a small child are too complicated for you to remember. I, your Creator, see the ways circumstances crippled you. I haven't forgotten one joy or one sorrow that you experienced. I know how these joys and sorrows have reached down through all the years of your life, freeing you, or binding you, making your heart sing, or making your heart cry. I know the healing that your life-tossed child soul needs. I can loose the tethers and free you from all that began to bind you from the moment you were conceived . . . for you were conceived from My heart . . . in My heart, and of My heart.
    With a father's love let Me dissolve all that binds you . . . let Me set you free! Let Me loosen the grips of crippling experiences.

Notes for Chapter Seven

1. Jack Dominian, *The Capacity to Love* (Darton, Longman and Todd, 1985) p. 13.
2. Jack Dominian, *The Capacity to Love*, p. 13.
3. Winnicott's phrase.
4. Edward Moss, *Growing Into Freedom* (Eagle, 1993) p. 8.
5. Keith Miller, *Habitation of Dragons* (Word Books, 1970) pp. 185–6.
6. Jack Dominian, *The Capacity to Love*, p. 74.
7. Edward Moss, *Growing into Freedom*, pp. 22–3.

8. Edward Moss, *Growing into Freedom*, p.11.
9. Francis MacNutt, *Healing* (Ave Maria Press, 1984) pp. 181–2.
10. Joyce Huggett, *Listening to Others* (Hodder and Stonghton, 1988).
11. George Appleton, *Prayers From a Troubled Heart* (Darton, Longman and Todd, 1983) p. 48.
12. Joan Hutson, *Heal My Heart, O Lord* (Ave Maria Press, 1976) p. 7.

8

BECOMING THE PERSON
GOD MADE ME TO BE

Inner healing and counselling need not compete with each
other. It is not unusual for a person gripped in the win-
ter of lovelessness to benefit from both. An experienced
Christian counsellor might use counselling skills during one
session and prayer ministry insights in another. Alternatively,
a psychotherapist might call on someone involved in prayer
ministry to work in partnership with him, the one working with
the client using therapeutic skills, and a pastor or other mature
Christian praying with the same client on other occasions. With
the client's permission, they will keep in touch with one another
until the client takes significant steps towards wholeness.

People like Alice, the little girl I mentioned who was so
emotionally battered during her childhood, may well need both
systematic counselling and inner healing if they are to be set
free to love in the way I described at the beginning of the last
chapter. She will neither find it easy to trust enough to receive
love again nor to take the risk of giving love. After all, she runs
the risk of being rejected all over again, and then what? Nor will
she find it easy to learn to communicate her truest feelings or
to co-operate with others in the way we see the members of
the Holy Trinity relating.

It may be that, with someone like Alice, another of the many
methods God uses to bring people into greater wholeness will
be the route he takes. For when a person has been so damaged
that they dare not lift the lid of Pandora's box for fear that the
past will somehow swamp them again, God gently woos them
with an undemanding healing touch. I think, for example, of the

prayer ministry which John Wimber, David and Mary Pytches, Leanne Payne and others have brought to our notice, as a result of which numerous emotionally crippled Christians have learned to love again.

This form of ministry differs from the method of inner healing I described in the last chapter, though technically this could also be called inner healing since it brings about a greater internal wholeness. It differs in this way. Instead of asking the person to go back, using the vividness of their imagination, to the place and time when they were wounded, and instead of asking the hurting person to picture Jesus in the scene as I did with Gill in chapter seven, we give the person the opportunity to share with us as much or as little of their story as seems appropriate, and then we make it clear that we are going to ask the Holy Spirit to fall upon them to do in them and for them whatever it is that he discerns is right at that moment. We invite the person simply to relax and to open themselves to receive God's Spirit. Then we call on the Holy Spirit to come in whatever way he should choose.

The person may not see anything in the way Gill saw the picture of God's hand holding the jewel. But very often they become aware of an indescribable overwhelming of the Spirit which is perhaps not unlike the way he overshadowed Mary when Jesus was conceived.

Just as that overshadowing produced the miracle of the Son of God's conception within a woman's womb, so the results of this kind of prayer suggest that deep, vital and lasting changes frequently occur.

Francis MacNutt quotes from a letter written to him by a woman he once prayed for in this way:

As you placed your hands very lightly on my forehead, a feeling of weightlessness came over me . . . There was this feeling of peace. Although I was semi-conscious, it was as if I were in another world which was very peaceful . . . so I just stayed there realizing for the first time in my life that Jesus loved me and forgave me my sins.[1]

Such testimonies are not rare. Such healing takes place frequently. It cannot be analysed or explained but it changes the lives of severely damaged people and brings them closer to discovering the person who lives inside them who has been trapped for decades by the haunting memories of past hurts.

Sometimes, as in the case of the woman Francis MacNutt mentions, when the Holy Spirit falls on a person in this way, the feeling of weightlessness referred to causes them to fall to the ground. As this woman put it in her letter:

'I got this feeling like I was falling and I could feel Father's hands grasping my head . . . Then I just went down like a feather, so softly. I felt weightlessness, but I was always conscious; I just had no control over my body.'[2]

Bible Meditation

When such healing comes, however it comes, it is like putting on a new pair of spectacles or suddenly hearing the first blackbird in Spring. And the years have shown me that, very often, the healing comes softly and gently, not when we are clamouring for it in a counselling session or a healing service, but when we least expect it, when we are on our own praying or meditating on a passage of Scripture or 'just being'.

That, at least, has been my experience.

In *Listening to Others*,[3] I have referred to my own birth trauma – how my mother went blind at my birth and the effect that had on my ability to love and be loved. In that same book, I referred to the healing which has trickled into my life over the years – through counselling and through prayer ministry. But inner healing, as I have said, is a process. It is as though God gives us as much healing as we need to bring us to a plateau from which we can live and relate with increasing freedom and maturity, and then surprises us with the joy of a fresh healing touch.

I have known the theory of this for many years but it had not occurred to me that my own healing process in this area was incomplete until I was meditating on Isaiah 66 on one occasion

some eighteen years after the first counselling session I had
received. This was what I read:

> Oh, that you may suck fully
> of the milk of her comfort,
> That you may nurse with delight
> at her abundant breasts.
> As nurslings, you shall be carried in her arms
> and fondled in her lap;
> As a mother comforts her [child],
> so will I comfort you.
>
> (Isaiah 66:11,12, JB)[4]

'Picture God as a comforting mother holding your inner child
close to her breasts,' suggested the author of the book I was
using to help me in my meditation. When I read that suggestion,
my first reaction was to recoil. Then I felt my heart freeze.
Something inside me refused to continue meditating. I closed
the book, put it down and, with a mighty heave, pushed away
the ambivalence which had risen unbidden to the surface of my
mind. I was overseas on a teaching tour at the time and faced a
busy day, so I spent the rest of my prayer time preparing myself
for the day ahead and thought no more about this curious act of
avoidance.

Two days later, however, while I was still 'coming to' as it
were after a good night's sleep, it was as though the bedroom
where I was staying was filled with the presence of God. It
almost seemed as though the Beloved had come through the
open window and enfolded me in tenderness. In fact, when I
tried to explain it later to the person in whose home I was
staying, I simply said: 'I had a visit from the Tender One this
morning,' and I remember being relieved when she asked no
questions but seemed to know what I meant.

I did not know that morning what I now know; that God
was preparing to take me on another lap of the journey
into wholeness. That morning, I simply luxuriated in the tender,
gentle, motherly love which enfolded me. Over the next few
days, while I stayed in that home, every morning started in the

same way: with the acute awareness of the enveloping presence of the Tender One. This continued for several days after I had left that place which had become holy ground for me. In the retreat house where I was leading the Easter retreat I referred to in Chapter Four, I was still conscious of the overshadowing of the Tender One. But then everything changed.

For no apparent reason, I found myself re-living, in my dreams and in my prayer times, the trauma of my birth. I was still on the teaching tour, still busy, still coping outwardly, but inwardly, I was in turmoil. At first, I thought the Tender One had deserted me but one warm, sunny day, as I sat on the shore of a lake trying to understand the inner turmoil and trying to spread it before God, the loving presence was there for me again – me the adult and me the baby. As memories of my birth flooded my memory yet again, I felt tender arms receiving me into the world and instinctively I knew that the deep inner wound which had been touched as I knelt at the foot of the Cross on Good Friday had been healed once and for all.

At first I failed to appreciate the connection between the visit of the Tender One and the exposure of this primal pain but during the retreat which sandwiched these two events, I 'happened' to discover a little book on the bookshelves of the retreat house: *The Way of Tenderness* by Kevin O'Shea. In it, he explains that tenderness

> is not something efficient, executive, managerial. It does not belong to the domain of getting things done. There is nothing violent in it, nothing strong in it. It is not manipulative, not task-oriented, not a thing of action. It belongs to being, rather than to doing, and to feeling, and to resting, in peace, at depth. It is a quality of being related, it is the limitlessness of being so, without strain or fear. There is something of love in it. It is the relaxedness that comes from knowing by experience that one is thoroughly and totally loved . . . If we could ask ourselves, 'at this very moment, right here, do I honestly believe that God likes me – not loves me, since He has to do that theologically, but likes me?' and if we could say,

'Yes He does,' and mean it, there would be a relaxedness and a gentleness with us that is close to what we are calling 'tenderness' . . . We could feel that we could love our whole life-story, that we are graced, and made beautiful, by the providence of our own history. That is what 'tenderness' might mean.[5]

The phrase, 'knowing by experience that one is thoroughly and totally loved,' and the sentence, 'We could feel that we could love our whole life-story,' seemed to sum up what I was experiencing, in greater depth than ever before. After I had pondered these insights, I read on.

The little booklet helped me to see that when we have experienced true tenderness, we are less afraid to come close to the pain and hurt which lies embedded in us. Instead of fighting it or denying it, we discover within us the resources to take 'a good, soft look at it'.[6] We can be calm about it, linger over it, not be overwhelmed by it. And we discover that it has lost some of its terror. Now that we have experienced true tenderness, the trauma seems, somehow, to be more manageable. There comes a moment of 'recognition' – a moment which proves to be constructive, creative, integrative and curiously healing. It is a quiet moment, a moment of intense and deep experience and awareness. Although we could not describe it in words, we are aware that it is having a profound effect on us. It is as though the safe boundaries we had set in place inside us were gradually dissolving. Yet we are at peace. Our whole being is touched, hushed, held.

We can remain at peace because tenderness opens our eyes to the reality that inner integration does not necessarily lie ahead of us in the realm of the 'not yet': 'It opens out to us a unity and an integrity we could never have claimed for ourselves, or found our path to arrive at it.'[7] But it is for now. And when our barriers melt inside us, our eyes refuse to focus fully on ourselves. Instead, we become more fully involved with the gift and the Giver. Instinctively, we trust both. They make us not so much vulnerable as transparent, that is, being consciously and completely open to a Presence which cannot and will not inflict hurt but which will, instead, touch totally the core of our being. Such is the level of our trust that we open more and more of ourselves to both the Giver and the gift. This is 'frailty smiled at'.[8] As we continue to unfold in the warmth of tenderness, we find ourselves able to befriend the dark depths of ourselves. When we do this, what we find in these hidden depths no longer masquerades as destructive forces but rather reveals themselves for what they are: qualities and events which can be redeemed and recycled.

With the wisdom of hindsight, as I reflect on the sequence of events which brought to me a greater degree of inner wholeness than I had previously encountered, I am once again awed by the depth and mystery of the love of the God whose longing is to set us free to become the people he created us to be.

The living word

In the climate in which we live, when scores of books have been written about counselling, inner healing and prayer ministry, it seems timely to underline that God's healing can and frequently does come in the quiet, undramatic moments when he encircles us with love – as we walk, as we work, as we contemplate the wonders of creation or as we meditate on the Scriptures. It is one of the reasons why, in Chapter Five, I stressed the importance of processing the fruit of our Bible meditation.

It happens not infrequently, for example, that we can be reading a familiar Gospel story or a passage like the one from Isaiah which I was reading that morning in my friend's house, when, if we are tuned in to our innermost self, we will detect an inner reaction or some strong feelings. If we listen to those emotions, moods and responses, they can point us to the need for inner healing. We may, for example, be meditating on the miracle Jesus performed at the Wedding at Cana in Galilee. While others might marvel at the way glimpses of his divinity shone through the young rabbi Jesus, we might detect within ourselves jealousy or anger or ambivalence towards Mary, or we might find ourselves hooked by the manner in which Jesus appears to have rebuked his mother on this occasion.

If we chide ourselves for harbouring unholy thoughts and feelings and, with a mighty effort, force ourselves to rejoice with the host of the wedding, we shall miss a golden opportunity. If, on the other hand, we will listen and talk to our jealousy, our anger or ambivalence, we may find ourselves being touched and healed by the Tender One.

Suppose we feel irritation with Mary who appears, to us, to be interfering. If we acknowledge this to ourselves and become a guest at that wedding, using the gift of the imagination in the way I described in Chapter Five, we may find ourselves talking to Jesus about this ambivalence. Perhaps we will ask him how he felt when his mother seemed to demand a miracle. Or maybe will find ourselves sympathising with him: 'Poor you! I know how that feels. My mother was always interfering too.' Or maybe the strength of our emotions will alarm us and we will find ourselves talking to Jesus about that. It could be that, if we are Protestants, we have been schooled to dismiss the role of Mary and that God will use this meditation to bring more balance into our view of the woman he chose to become the mother of his Son.

No one can predict ahead of time what the outcome of such a meditation might be. But if painful, inhibiting memories are triggered by praying with Scripture, these should not be pushed to one side. They need to be confronted and prayed over until our hearts are healed.

Healing might well come to us if we return more than once to this story of the Wedding at Cana. As we do so, we recall where we left off our conversation with Jesus last time and start our prayer by resuming the conversation at that point, in the same way as we might address a friend. We do this until, intuitively, we know that this passage has shown us all we need to know at this stage of our pilgrimage. Alternatively, or as a follow-up, we turn to John 19: 25–7 and watch and learn from the way Jesus relates to his mother there:

'Standing near the cross were Jesus' mother, Mary, his

aunt, the wife of Cleopas, and Mary Magdalene. When Jesus saw his mother standing there beside me, his close friend, he said to her, "He is your son." And to me he said, "She is your mother!" And from then on I took her into my home' (LB).

As we stand there, still recalling perhaps the conversations we have already had with Jesus about our relationship with our mother, we might allow him to draw from us any bitterness or resentment which we recognise we are still harbouring. Or we might find our hardness towards our own mother melting as we contemplate Jesus's example. Despite his own anguish of body, mind and spirit, he forgets himself and concentrates, instead, on his mother's urgent need of friendship and human love. So he gives her his closest friend as companion, confidante and comforter.

As Gerard Hughes observes in *God of Surprises*, the effect such prayer can have is astonishing, lifting heavy burdens from people's lives, 'bringing back to them a capacity for joy and delight in life which may have been stifled for years and, in some cases, restoring to physical health people who had been suffering for years from illnesses which did not respond to medical treatment.'9

Deliverance

The Holy Spirit sometimes uses this kind of meditation to deliver us from the negativity which would prevent us from becoming the person he created us to be.

Like the young man who once described for me what had happened while he was meditating on the raising of Lazarus. He related how, in his imagination, he had 'become' Lazarus lying in the grave of his felt lovelessness. While lying there, the voice of Jesus pierced the darkness of the grave and of his consciousness: 'Lazarus, come out!' (John 11:43, LB). He obeyed. Still wrapped in his grave clothes, he hobbled to the entrance of the tomb and stood waiting at the foot of the flight of stairs which separated him from Jesus and his sisters: 'But as I came out of the darkness, all kinds of other things rushed out in front of me,' he said, 'like snakes and rats. It was as though I was not only being given a brand new start in life, but at the same time, God was ridding me of all the negativity which had been polluting my life for years: hatred and bitterness, resentment and jealousy.'

He then went on to tell me what had happened when Jesus invited the by-standers to 'Unwrap him and let him go!' (John 11:44, LB). He found himself valuing and responding to the tenderness with which his sisters and friends removed the bandages which still bound him: 'That's symbolic too. I know my negativity has prevented me from reaching out to others in love but this encounter with Christ has given me new hope and the courage to start again.'

I was deeply moved by this testimony for two reasons. One, because I sensed that God had silently and secretly exercised what is sometimes called 'the deliverance ministry'. And two, because of the role played by the sisters and friends in the medi- tation. We look at these in turn. First, the deliverance ministry.

Deliverance Ministry

Francis MacNutt defines this as 'a process, mainly through prayer, of freeing a person who is *oppressed* by evil spirits'.[10] He draws an important destinction between possession and oppression, making it clear that the deliverance ministry is not the same as exorcism. He admits to trying to avoid any involvement with the ministry of deliverance but found himself a practitioner because, as he puts it in *Healing*: 'there were some people I simply could not help merely by praying for inner healing. Prayer for deliverance sometimes was called for.'[11]

He highlights some of the indications that deliverance ministry may be needed instead of, or as well as, the prayer for inner healing. One is that the prayer for inner healing seems to accomplish nothing. He explains:

I have come to expect that prayer for inner healing will ordinarily have a perceptible effect. If, after prayer, a person says, 'I still have a feeling of being tied up inside,' it may indicate a need for further counselling or support in community, or more prayer for inner healing – or, possibly, for deliverance.[12]

He highlights, too, the differences between the prayer for deliverance and the prayer for healing:

1. Whereas prayer for healing is addressed to God, a prayer of deliverance . . . is directed to the oppressing demons.
2. Whereas prayer for healing is ordinarily a petition, prayer for deliverance is a *command* . . . to the demonic forces, ordering them to depart in the name of Jesus Christ, as did Paul to the spirit influencing the soothsaying girl: 'I order you in the name of Jesus Christ to come out of her' (Acts 16:18b).[13]

I have found, when exercising this kind of ministry, that there is no need to shout or rant or rave. There is a need to be as firm as we might be with a yapping dog when we round on it with an authoritative 'Be quiet!' I have also found that, before embarking on this ministry, we need to beg God for the gift of discernment lest we minister inappropriately and do more harm than good.

But, like Francis MacNutt, I have also discovered that there are people whose need for healing is urgent but who are incapable of receiving it because they are blocked by the demonic. Like the girl I once prayed for on one of our overseas trips. She had been describing for me the hatred and bitterness with which she seemed consumed and, together, we had prayed for the healing of her heart. In the middle of the prayer, it became apparent that, before she could receive healing, she needed deliverance. I simply commanded, in the Name of the Lord Jesus Christ, that the bitterness and hatred should depart. She coughed a choked kind of cough and then clung to me as she said: 'Something's gone . . . It went over there,' she added, pointing to a nearby swimming pool. 'I feel suddenly free.' She was free. Free to receive the healing she needed to turn her back on years of compulsive bitterness so that she could learn to love again.

The role of friends

One of the reasons God brings us into healing is so that we may learn to relate to others in the way I described at the beginning of the last chapter: in the way the three members of the Holy Trinity love, co-operate and communicate with each other. Is that why God almost always brings someone else alongside us when he heals our hearts, I wonder?

The fact of the matter is that other people are almost always given the privilege of incarnating for us the healing love which is being applied to our heart's hurts by the Holy Spirit. Sometimes, as we have seen, the person is a highly qualified counsellor or psychotherapist. At other times, it is someone who has been entrusted with the sensitivity and gifts required to pray for inner healing for others. On other occasions it is a skilled spiritual director who is trained and experienced in discerning the movement of God's Spirit in us. And sometimes it is close friends or relatives – those capable of embodying for us the tenderness which flows from the Tender One but which we need to feel in human form.

As Kevin O'Shea explains, the tenderness which gives rise to the re-birth of trust begs to be shared: 'There is no way of keeping reserved or enclosed what is by nature transparent. It is already *an overture to others*. This overture is the beginning of a new kind of trust in others.'[14]

He goes on to explain the importance of this re-orientation. Before the healing touch was felt, we operated from a place of inner hurt behind the defences which we had built to protect ourselves from being injured further. As the defences dissolve, a new 'self' emerges, a 'self' more like the person we were created to be. Consequently, we grow in our awareness of who we are by grace and by the changes which are taking place inside us. Our need for a person or people with whom to share this new 'self' is urgent. It is as we share that we mature and are assured that another can resonate to the same tenderness. It is in the face, the smile, the eyes, the touch, the embrace of another that the fruit of this tenderness matures. It does not mature suddenly or quickly – but slowly and sometimes with a struggle. Like the lemon tree in my garden. In its first season, four years ago, it was the proud bearer of one lemon. Then it appeared to have died. Yet we detected signs of life. The more the tree battled, the more we cared for it – fertilising the soil around it, watering it, talking to it, cherishing it. Now, at last, it is showing promising signs of growth and we have every hope of fruit next year.

God, similarly, watches over our progress and yearns, for our sakes, that we will bear the fruit of the tenderness and healing with which he fertilises and waters our lives. And when the fruit does appear, we shall find within ourselves an ever-increasing capacity to become the loving and lovable people God created us to be.

For personal reflection

1. Read the following poem:

> My friend . . .
> you who are part of me
> please take away the veil
> that covers me – please set me free.
>
> You know that we belong, are deeply one.
> I cannot see you clearly
> there is this veil,
> that covers heart and mind and soul.
>
> Did people put it there
> or did I choose this cover
> To protect, to hide
> my insecurity, my wounded self?

Or is it just the final skin
of my unfinished birth
to personhood, to self
which you possess already?

Please take it off with tender care;
I am so insecure, so easily hurt.
Your love can set me free.
Your trust will melt my veil.

Then we can fully meet
in giving and receiving
in seeing, understanding.
We will be whole and free and one.

In oneness we will look
into the world, towards people, God,
uplifting many veils
and freeing hidden beauty – life.

2. Look back over your life and recall the people who have
   lifted your many veils. Thank God for them. If they are
   still alive, you might like to write to some of them or thank
   them on the telephone.
3. Write a prayer in your journal thanking God for bringing
   these friends and mentors across your path.

Notes for Chapter Eight

1. Francis MacNutt, *Overcome by the Spirit* (Eagle, 1991) p. 37.
2. Francis MacNutt, *Overcome by the Spirit*, p. 37.
3. Joyce Huggett, *Listening to Others* (Hodder and Stoughton, 1988).
4. Quoted Mary Meehan SSC, *Exploring the Feminine Face of God* (Sheed and Ward, 1991) p. 63.
5. Kevin O'Shea CSSR, *The Way of Tenderness* (Paulist Press, 1978) pp. 9–10.
6. Kevin O'Shea CSSR, *The Way of Tenderness*, p. 11.
7. Kevin O'Shea CSSR, *The Way of Tenderness*, p. 14.
8. Kevin O'Shea CSSR, *The Way of Tenderness*, p. 19.

 9. Gerard Hughes SJ, *God of Surprises* (Darton, Longman and Todd, 1986) p. 86.
10. Francis MacNutt, *Healing* (Ave Maria Press, 1984) p. 208.
11. Francis MacNutt, *Healing*, p. 209.
12. Francis MacNutt, *Healing*, p. 217.
13. Francis MacNutt, *Healing*, p. 218.
14. Kevin O'Shea CSSR, *The Way of Tenderness*, p. 19.
15. Henry Rohr, *Set Me Free* (Spectrum Publications, 1972).

9

FREE TO LOVE

Even though we may have been emotionally wounded on numerous occasions, when we begin to yield to the healing touch of the Tender One, our view of the world and of ourselves will begin to change. Among other things, perhaps for the first time in our lives, we may find ourselves believing that we have been created in the image of God; that he has adopted us into his family; that just as every child in a human family is unique, with its own distinct personality, its own set of fingerprints and its own way of loving its parents, so, too, we are unique to God and the world. We shall begin to warm to the description of ourselves as 'friends of God' (Exodus 33:11; John 15:14) and recognise that, just as God once said to Moses, 'there is a place near me where you may stand' (Exodus 33:21), so there is a special place at his side ear-marked for us.

And some of the Bible's other pen-pictures will take on new meaning for us. Like Paul's picture of the body of Christ in 1 Corinthians 12:12–31, for example. We shall discern that, through Paul, God is underlining that, as the song puts it, 'each child is special, accepted and loved, a love gift from Jesus from his Father above', and that that 'specialness' includes us. We shall be able to look in the mirror as well as into the inner recesses of our being and echo the Psalmist's awed hymn of praise:

You created *my* inmost being;
you knit *me* together in my mother's womb.
I praise you because I am fearfully and wonderfully made;
your works are wonderful

(Psalm 139:13, my emphasis)

We shall even be able to add our personal, authentic, resounding 'Amen' to this prayer:

> Lord my God, when your love spilled over
> into creation
> You thought of me.
> I am
> from love   of love   for love.[1]

And when we are assured that, indeed, we are from love and of love, then an important foundation stone will have been laid in our lives on which we can build for the future. We shall be ready to make the life-long experiential exploration into what it means to have been created 'for love'.

Jesus's love

The true meaning of the word 'love' has not only been devalued over the centuries, it has been almost eroded. That is why, in this chapter, we place the spotlight on Love incarnate, love in human flesh, Jesus himself. He is the only person who has lived on earth who has personified love in all its purity, so he is the only one qualified to show us how to become the loving and lovable people we were created to be.

Love is what God is. So when Jesus lived on earth, love flowed out of him in ever-expanding concentric circles. At the centre of those circles, after he had left his home in Nazareth, we see him relating intimately with one person: John the beloved. From that smallest circle of love spread a bigger one, his relationships with the privileged three: Peter, James and John. But these close relationships were by no means exclusive. From them emerged an even bigger circle which embraced the Twelve, and after that the circles of love seemed limitless, drawing in friends like Lazarus, Martha and Mary, Mary Magdalene, Salome, 'the women from Galilee' who supported Jesus with their presence as well as their presents, beggars, lepers, widows, children . . . The list is endless. In other words, it would appear that, in his earthly ministry, Jesus did not love everyone with the same degree of intensity, even though his love embraced everyone. It would also appear that he chose carefully and prayerfully those with whom he would relate most closely, and that he chose not independence but interdependence as the base from which he would establish his Kingdom. Clearly, just as his Father once pronounced, 'It isn't good for man to be alone' (Genesis 2:18 LB), so Jesus recognised that inter-relatedness and inter-connectedness with others was vital to his wholeness and effectiveness.

Was this the reason why he retreated to the hills for a whole night of prayer prior to selecting the Twelve? We are not told. It would appear, however, that when he returned from that nocturnal retreat, there was no doubt in his mind that there were twelve particular men with whom God wanted him to live in community. We also know that the principle of the concentric circles is an important one for us if we are to become the loving people God created us to be. John Powell paints the picture helpfully and persuasively:

'I cannot enter into a love-relationship with many people. I would be exhausted in the effort. So I must choose . . . Since love can exist on many levels, it is extremely important not to offer a commitment of love which I may not be able to honour.'[2]

We, too, must therefore make choices. Such choices should be made, not in the heat of the moment, but after careful thought and prayer. Certain probing questions sometimes help us in the selection process. The first is a particularly penetrating one:

'Am I squeezing relationships into my spare time or are they the base from which I work?'

There are five more:

1. 'What do I want from this relationship and what can I give to it?'
2. 'Within the apparent givenness of my profession or vocation, if I am realistic, how much time do I have to forge close friendships?'

3. 'To whom do I owe my primary commitment?'
4. 'Whom else do I love and in what way?'
5. 'What are the demands on my time and energy to which I must fully respond in order to become fully myself?'

Although on paper this may look rather cold and clinical, it is important to confront such questions, particularly before embarking on any new close relationship. John Powell outlines the possible consequences of failing to do this:

> Most people lurk behind protective walls . . . 'security operations'. These are designed to protect an already injured ego from further vulnerability. At the call of love, these people come out, perhaps haltingly at first, but they do come out, reassured by the promises of love. If I have made a premature or overstated commitment, I will later have to take back my promises made to such a person. I will have to explain that I really did not mean what I said or that I have changed my mind. I will leave that person standing painfully naked and unprotected. He will . . . go back behind a higher and more impenetrable wall. And, once burned, doubly cautious, it may be a long time before anyone will ever successfully call him out again, if that be possible at all.[3]

A close, committed love

Jesus did not make that cruel mistake. Having made his careful, prayerful choice of friends, he dedicated himself wholeheartedly to making the relationships work. Even though his chosen ones misunderstood him,[4] challenged him,[5] quarrelled with each other,[6] and let him down,[7] he loved them to the end.

He was so committed to them that he made himself available to them. He did this by reading their hearts:

'There was no need for anyone to tell him about them because he himself knew what was in their hearts' (John 2:25 GNB).

He not only read them, he felt for them, and created the warm, accepting climate where they could discover what it meant to be privileged children of the Kingdom.

His concern for and promotion of their growth was typically Middle Eastern. It was expressed through the intimacy of loving looks, affectionate touch and warm words. As a born and bred Westerner, it is good for me to live in the Middle East and encounter local Christians publicly expressing their love for one another. I think, for example, of the retreat my husband and I were leading just before I settled down to write this chapter. Most of the retreatants came from the Middle East. God had drawn us very close to one another during our short time together. So, as the retreat drew to its close, it seemed natural for the men to sit with their arms around each other, enjoying to the full this non-erotic touch. It seemed natural, too, for the women to embrace each other, not with a quick hug, but with long, leisurely, loving embraces.

Jesus is a model for this kind of intimacy. He was unafraid to express affection. John reminds us that, at the Last Supper, he 'was reclining next to him' (John 13:23). When Jesus warned them that one of them would betray him, his distress was clear for all to see.

Simon seems to have motioned John to ask Jesus which of them was to turn traitor, whereupon John leaned back against Jesus (v. 25). Again, here in the Middle East, that would seem neither inappropriate nor unseemly. No one would recoil from such demonstrations of affectionate understanding: rather they would recognise that, with John, Jesus is simply modelling warm, affectionate, non-genital, same-sex loving.

But, contrary to his culture, he expressed, openly and in public, love across the sex divide as well. Luke records how, on one occasion, while Jesus was dining with Simon, the Pharisee, a prostitute approached him with her heart obviously brim-full with love for him. This love overflowed in the form of tears as she knelt at his feet. Her tears washed his feet, so she wiped them, not with a towel but with her long, flowing hair. Then she anointed them with the expensive perfume she had brought as a gift for him (Luke 7:36–8). When Simon poured scorn on the woman's actions, Jesus defended her, highlighting and applauding the genuineness of her love and contrasting it with Simon's seeming hostility and lack of hospitality.

Warm, genuine, tactile, verbal love. This is the pattern of Jesus's love. The Holy Spirit's task is to set us free to love like that.

People in the West, as I have hinted, may find that it takes time for them to learn to feel comfortable with non-erotic touch. But, as Joyce Rupp explains in *Praying Our Goodbyes*:

> Touch fills a person's being with the energy of bonding and love. Without ever saying a word, the message is given: 'I care. I am here for you. Here is some strength of mine to go on; here is some love to energize you when you need it so much.' Touch connects one to another in care, makes contact with heartache . . . warms the cold or exhausted spirit. Touch can penetrate barriers of despair, anguish, hardness or bitterness.[8]

Words and looks

Jesus's love was expressed, not only in touch, but also in looks and words. What did Peter read in the Lord's eyes in the courtyard on that unforgettable Good Friday? The Bible does not tell us, so we can only guess. Could it have been hurt love, the pain a person feels when a dear friend has rejected him? And what did the woman caught in the act of adultery see in Jesus's eyes? Again, the Bible remains silent. Could it have been accepting love? What did Mary and John see in Jesus's blood-shot eyes as he hung from the Cross? Undoubtedly, tender, suffering but generous love.

Though we are left to draw our own conclusions about what people saw shining through Jesus's eyes, the Bible makes it patently clear that Jesus was a man who was unafraid to vocalise the love which he felt for his disciples. Take the conversation he had with them in the Upper Room, for example. Here he repeatedly tells and shows them just how deep and extensive his love for them is:

'As the Father has loved me, so have I loved you' (John 15:9).

Did John remind the disciples of this amazing declaration of love during those agonising hours sandwiched between Christ's Crucifixion and that sensitive Resurrection appearance in that same Upper Room on Resurrection Day? Did they deliberate on the other references he made to his love for them – such as:

'Love one another *as I have loved you*? (John 15:12, my emphasis).

Or did they remind each other that he made comments like this more than once?

'As I have loved you, so you must love one another' (John 13:34).

Again, we are not told. What is clear, however, is that Jesus felt uninhibited about expressing the love he felt for people. We will know that we are becoming the people God created us to be, that is, those formed in the image of his all-loving Son, when we, too, grow in our capacity to give love and to receive it. For some of us, as we have observed in a previous chapter, this may take a long time, so we shall have to exercise patience, contrasting Jesus's example with that of an elderly man I once read about.

This man had a close friend with whom he lived in a Christian community. Over the years they had learned to understand each other, empathise with each other and support each other. When one was sick, the other was there, available to him. Or when one had good news to share, the other was there, entering into his joy. One day, unexpectedly and tragically, one of the men was run over by a car in the road opposite the community's home. He was killed instantly. As soon as his friend heard the news, he rushed into the street, knelt beside his friend's body, wrapped his arms around him and cried: 'Wake up! You can't die yet. I never told you that I loved you.'

Affirmation

Jesus *did* tell his friends how much he loved them. He also demonstrated this love in non-verbal ways. For example, he affirmed them.

Jack Dominian reminds us that 'the word affirmation comes from the Latin "affirmare" and it means to make firm, to give strength to . . . the human personality'.[9] He also explains what affirmation does, suggesting that it answers two questions which are pertinent to the subject of this book. The questions are:

'Who am I?'

'What do I mean to myself in relation to myself and others?'

Affirmation helps us to find the solutions to these questions in a variety of ways. When someone reflects back to us the way they value and appreciate us, they increase our sense of self-worth and therefore help us to discover who we really are. And when someone increases our sense of self-worth, they give us a priceless gift – the awareness that we are full of potential, some clues to help us identify the specific nature of that potential, and therefore some hints to help us find an answer to the second question: 'What do I mean to myself in relation to myself and others?'

Notice the way Jesus did this for Peter. Before Peter had even started to serve his apprenticeship with Jesus, and while he was still protesting his unworthiness to keep company with the Master, he heard these affirming words pouring from the Lord's lips:

'Don't be afraid [Simon], from now on you will catch men' (Luke 5:10b). In other words, Simon, you have a unique role to play in the Kingdom.

Even more astonishingly, many months later, yet more affirmation came Peter's way as Jesus gave him a new symbolic name:

'You are Peter, and on this rock I will build my church' (Matthew 16:18).

Up to this point, Peter's track record had not been particularly impressive and, as time went on, it was to grow steadily worse. He was the one who acted as the mouth-piece of those trying to dissuade Jesus from travelling to Jerusalem. He was the one who, during the Last Supper, refused to allow Jesus to wash his feet. He was the one who would deny Jesus three times. But Jesus detected his potential and carefully and sensitively drew this out. In doing so, in the language of John Powell, Jesus was underlining Peter's value as 'an unique, unrepeatable and even sacred mystery of humanity'.[10]

Assumed responsibility for people

One of the reasons why Jesus possessed this great capacity for affirming others was that he loved from a healed rather than from a hurting centre. This, in turn, gave him the inner freedom and space, not only to read people's hearts, but to recognise and meet their needs. To meet the needs of another is 'the fruit of friendship'.[11] It is one of the many faces of love, for love not only gives itself to others, it walks a mile in another's moccasins, to quote the old Indian proverb, and through empathy, discerns their real needs. At the same time, love remains separate from the need in order to make itself available to the needy person without being overwhelmed by them.

Was this the reason why, in Mark 1, for example, when Jesus's disciples sought him out insisting that he should leave that prayer-saturated place to return to the clamouring crowds, Jesus made the astonishing suggestion: 'Let's go somewhere else'?

We cannot know for certain what prompted that decision. We must, however, recognise that, if we are to love effectively, we too must set boundaries and refuse to be in bondage to the person in need. This is what Jesus modelled. In doing so, he gave his friends the greatest gift anyone can give another: 'the gift of belovedness'. I never cease to marvel at the methods Jesus used to give his closest friends this gift.

I think, for example, of those gruelling hours leading to his arrest in the Garden of Gethsemane. Although, during the Last Supper, he must have experienced a great deal of personal anguish, with painstaking care he prepared his disciples for the shock and trauma of their forthcoming bereavement:

'Do not let your hearts be troubled . . . In my Father's house are many rooms; if it were not so, I would have told you. I am going there to prepare a place for you. And if I go and prepare a place for you, I will come back and take you to be with me that you also may be where I am' (John 14:1–3).

This self-giving love which detected and ministered to the inner needs of the loved one was in evidence after the Resurrection also. Think of Mary weeping at the empty tomb. Jesus saw. Jesus cared. Jesus came. With one, economical, power-filled word he consoled her: 'Mary' (John 20:16). Or think of Thomas. Into the empty shell of his doubt, the risen Lord came with the much-needed invitation:

'Put your finger here; see my hands. Reach out your hand and put it into my side. Stop doubting and believe' (John 20:27).

Forgiveness

Even more astonishingly, perhaps, Jesus forgave his failing friends. The Greek word for 'to forgive' is *aphesis*. It is the word Jesus used at the grave of Lazarus. Having called Lazarus from the tomb, he invites the by-standers to *aphesis* – that is, to set him free from the grave-clothes so that he can go. In other words, 'to forgive' actually means 'to let go', 'to drop'.

This is precisely what we see Jesus doing in his relationships with his disciples. They failed him so many times. Although they lived with him and listened to his teaching, they failed to understand the true nature of his mission. Even at the Last Supper, some of them were arguing about which of them would be the greatest in Christ's Kingdom. Worse was to come when, instead of supporting him through the agonising hours of his arrest, trial and crucifixion, they deserted him.

Jesus was human. He must surely have been hurt by their rejection and neglect. Yet, on the first Easter Day, he made it clear that he was clinging to no grudges, no resentment, no hatred. Rather, he was ready to reach out to them in love.

On my desk, as I write, lies a photograph of a statue which stands on a small beach on the shores of the Sea of Galilee – the spot where it is believed Jesus re-commissioned Peter. As I have been gazing at this picture, I have been trying to place myself in Peter's shoes. If the other disciples had failed their Lord, he was the failure *par excellence*. Not only had he deserted Jesus, like all the rest, he had denied that he even knew this man he so fervently loved. Did he have trouble looking the Resurrected Jesus in the eye, I wonder? Did he shuffle along the beach shamefacedly? We are not told. But we know that Jesus did not humiliate him in any way. On the contrary, he seemed eager to restore this leader designate of the early church. Just as Peter had denied him three times, now Jesus gives him three opportunities to declare his love. Then Jesus commissions him – feed my sheep, feed my lambs.

Peter's posture in this picture before me speaks of unworthiness, helplessness and renewed commitment. He kneels at Jesus's feet with one hand held out in despair while the other is receiving the shepherd's crook which Jesus is handing to him. The figure of Jesus, on the other hand, exudes tenderness, trust and tranquil strength.[12] Qualities I imagine we shall enjoy as we become more and more like the warm, affectionate, affirming, forgiving people he made us to be.

Transparency

But Jesus's loving of his disciples and friends was memorable, not just because of what he did for them, but also because of who he was. Most of us, as we have already seen, defend ourselves with masks. Many of us carry around, as it were, a brief-case full of them so that we can change them as circumstances demand.

Jesus, on the other hand, was transparent. He revealed both personal strengths and personal limitations. There were times, for example, when his divinity peeped through his humanity – as when he changed the water into wine at the Wedding at Cana in Galilee. There were times, too, when his divinity streamed through – as on the Mount of Transfiguration. But there were other occasions when he was transparently weak and helpless: at his birth, for example, or as he stumbled under the weight of his Cross on the Via Dolorosa.

There were other limitations also. When James and John made their request for preferential treatment in the Kingdom, Jesus replied: 'I do not have the right to choose who will sit at my right and my left. It is God who will give these places to those for whom he has prepared them' (Mark 10:40, GNB). In other words, Jesus was a man under authority, a man in submission, a man with set limits and yet one who was gloriously free – the person his Father created him to be.

What was the secret of his transparency? What kind of person is it who detects the strengths in others and affirms them? What kind of person is it who is more concerned for the welfare of the loved one than his own well-being? What kind of person is it who readily forgives? What kind of person is it who has no need to project a psuedo-self; who clearly states what his limitations are? If we can discover the answers to those questions, we may draw a little closer to discovering who it is we are intended to be.

As we study the life-style of Jesus, it becomes clear that the person who loves in this way enjoys a double sense of security. Such people are secure in the love of God and therefore secure in their God-given identity. Jesus seems to have reached this enviable, liberating state by the age of twelve! So, in Luke 2:46–9, we see him in the temple, able to hold his own with the teachers of the Law, a poised, secure, purposeful youth who had already discovered his mission in life. As he expressed it to Mary and Joseph, 'I must be busy with my Father's affairs' (Luke 2:49, JB). He had had a normal, village home life in Nazareth where doubtless he experienced the warmth of human parenting from Mary and Joseph, but now he had reached the stage of maturity where, unashamedly, he could separate himself from them and insist on the appropriateness of establishing himself as his own person in relationship with his heavenly Father and the world at large. He was not rejecting his parents; indeed, he remained 'obedient to them' (Luke 2:51, LB). But he refused to remain in bondage to them.

We will know that we are more like the person God created us to be when we, too, refuse to remain in bondage to anyone: parents, the past, friends, culture. We will also recognise that we are becoming increasingly free when we, too, feel sufficiently secure in God, in ourselves and about ourselves, that we can affirm others and extend to them warm, accepting love.

In Cyprus a phrase which is often used is, 'Slowly, slowly!'

And because we are novices in this art-form of loving, it is a phrase we need to whisper to ourselves while we learn this particular skill. That is why I value Antoine de Saint-Exupéry's charming story, *The Little Prince*.

In this book, a prince from another planet visits planet earth. While on earth, he finds himself gripped by loneliness. Until, one day, he meets a fox:

> 'Come and play with me,' proposed the little prince, 'I am so unhappy.'
>
> 'I cannot play with you,' the fox said, 'I am not tamed.' . . .
>
> 'What does that mean – "tame"?'
>
> 'It is an act too often neglected,' said the fox. 'It means to establish ties.'
>
> '"To establish ties"?'
>
> 'Just that,' said the fox. 'To me, you are still nothing more than a little boy who is just like a hundred thousand other little boys. And I have no need of you. And you, on your part, have no need of me. To you, I am nothing more than a fox like a hundred thousand other foxes. But if you tame me, then we shall need each other. To me, you will be unique in all the world. To you, I shall be unique in all the world . . .'
>
> 'What must I do, to tame you?' asked the little prince.
>
> 'You must be be very patient,' replied the fox. 'First you will sit down at a little distance from me – like that – in the grass. I shall look at you out of the corner of my eye, and you will say nothing . . . But you will sit a little closer to me, every day . . .' The next day the prince came back . . .
>
> So the little prince tamed the fox.[13]

Just as the little prince tamed the fox, so Jesus tamed his disciples. After they had lived with Jesus for three years, the disciples were fast reaching the stage when they could tame each other.

A touching scene in the musical *Godspell* highlighted this.

Many Christians, myself included, were disturbed by the portrayal of the person of Jesus in this musical, but the scene I refer to was a powerful one.

It is the Last Supper. Jesus has washed his disciples' feet. He prepares for the final farewells. He moves around the table, embracing, kissing or playfully ruffling the hair of one disciple after another. Then he does a curious thing. He holds up a mirror in front of each of the disciples in turn. As he does so, the disciple's make-up is removed – not by the disciple himself but by his neighbour.

This was a moment of great significance. To allow someone else to wipe off the make-up which masks our real self requires a great deal of trust. And if we are to become the loving and lovable, maskless people God created us to be, we must be lured out of the false security of life behind the mask and take the risk of allowing others to discover who we really are. This interdependence modelled to us by Jesus transforms us. No one has taught me this more clearly than Chris.

When Chris first came to see me, he was one of the loneliest people I had ever encountered. He was in his late twenties but had only ever experienced even a modicum of closeness with one other person in his entire life. This friend, a flat-mate, had just moved, leaving Chris bereft. The pain of separation seemed unbearable. When he came to see me, he gave voice to his feelings of loss and bereavement. We invited God to come into the lonely void. And we looked at Chris's circle of acquaintances. Where could he, a single, shy introvert, find security, warmth and a place to belong? He doubted whether he could take the risk of reaching out to others again. I happened to know of a church in the town where Chris lived and suggested he tried it. Three months later, he visited me again. I scarcely recognised him. His eyes were shining. He smiled. He was full of news about his fulfilling job and the new church.

'Chris. You're so different. What's happened?'

He laughed. 'It's the house group at that church you suggested I should try. The services on Sunday aren't at all what I'm used to but the house group is great. They were pleased to see me, welcomed me and even looked out for me on Sundays at church. They're so friendly that I feel wanted, accepted and even appreciated. I didn't know it could be like this.

The members of that house group were probably totally unaware that they were taming Chris – becoming instruments of God's healing for him. Yet they conveyed to him the message we all need to hear:

'I am lovable! I don't have to do anything or be anything but myself.'[14]

In this way, they drew him out of his self-protecting fortress and set him free to give and receive love again. When people do this for us so that the 'I am lovable' message is etched on our hearts, then we are free to serve.

For personal reflection

1. Recall the claim that Jesus's ministry flowed from the relationships he established. Compare this with your own philosophy and life-style.
2. Write a prayer out of the experience.
3. Take a fresh look at the six questions on pp. 125–6, and spend time reflecting on them and answering them.
4. What has the experience shown you about yourself? Do you need to make changes in your life-style or relationships? What are you going to do about this?
5. Write a prayer asking the Holy Spirit to continue to transform you into the loving and lovable person God created you to be.

Notes for Chapter Nine

1. Jacqueline Syrup Bergan and S. Marie Schwan, *Love: A Guide for Prayer* (Saint Mary's Press, Minnesota, 1985) p. 11.
2. John Powell, *The Secret of Staying in Love* (Argus Books, 1974) p. 48.
3. John Powell, *The Secret of Staying in Love*, p. 48.
4. Luke 18:34.
5. Luke 8:45.
6. Luke 22:24.
7. Luke 22:46.

8. Joyce Rupp, *Praying Our Goodbyes* (Ave Maria Press, 1991) p. 91.
9. Jack Dominian, *Cycles of Affirmation* (Darton, Longman and Todd, 1977) p. 154.
10. John Powell, *The Secret of Staying in Love*, p. 56.
11. Henri Nouwen's phrase.
12. This photograph has been reproduced in my book, *The Smile of Love* (Hodder and Stoughton, 1990).
13. Antoine de Saint-Exupéry, *The Little Prince* (Piccolo, 1982) pp. 63–6.
14. John Powell, *The Secret of Staying in Love*, p. 19.

10

FREE TO SERVE

Until we know who we are and what our gifts are, we cannot discover how we might most effectively make an impact for Christ in our small corner of the universe. We might even find zealous, well-meaning Christian leaders or peers steering us towards ministries for which we are ill-equipped. And that would be a tragedy because, when every part of our being responds to the orchestration of the Spirit, a surge of energy seems to flow through us and thrill us in rather the same way as musicians thrill to the harmony they are helping to create.

One reason for this tremendous surge of energy is that when we allow God to conduct our lives, we enjoy a foretaste of heaven and we catch a glimpse of the person he created us to be. Paul put it this way: we were created 'to praise the glory of his [God's] grace' (Ephesians 1:6, JB).

The catechism on which Christians used to be reared put it another way:

'God made me to know him, love him and serve him in this world and to be happy with him in the world to come.'

The contemporary author, Gerard Hughes, commenting on the same theme, writes:

'Before the world was made we were chosen to live in love in God's presence by praising, reverencing and serving him in and through creation.'[1]

The Book of Common Prayer draws the seemingly paradoxical conclusion that 'his service is perfect freedom'.

In other words, when we serve God we are truly free because he created us in such a way that we will only enjoy complete fulfilment in life when we are reverencing him and everyone and everything he has made, and when we are serving him and them. This lies at the very heart of who we are.

The big lie

There is a snag, however. As children of our first parents, Adam and Eve, we have become victims of the Fall.

Just as our first parents believed the big lie Satan whispered in their ears – that God is a spoil-sport, out to deprive us of joy rather than to delight us with his love, so we are easily beguiled into believing in this caricature of God. This means that a civil war may frequently rage inside us. While some parts of our personality will struggle to be true to our calling, to serve Christ and the world, to serve Christ in the world, other parts of us will rebel and insist on putting self before our Master. One of the challenges which faces us, therefore, is to discern and to discipline those parts of ourselves which seem intent on ensuring that our world revolves around 'number one', self, rather than God.

Someone has suggested that the way to do this is to become like the woman who owned two dogs: one white and one black. These dogs used to fight frequently and ferociously. But over a period of time, a friend of the woman observed that while one week the white dog would win the fight, the following week the victor would be the black dog. Because the pattern persisted with monotonous regularity, the friend could contain her curiosity no longer so she asked the dog's owner if there was an obvious reason for this pattern. Whereupon her friend explained that the answer was simple: 'One week I feed the white dog and starve the black one, while the following week, I feed the black one and starve the white. The dog which is being fed is the one which wins.' We, similarly, need to ensure that, while the God-pleasing, God-serving part of our personality is fed and nurtured and therefore strengthened, the narcissistic parts of our personality are gradually starved into defeat.

Saying 'Yes' to God

That is not to imply, however, that the main initiative in winning this perennial battle is ours. It is not. God takes the initiative. I discovered this while I was on retreat on one occasion. One of the questions I had taken with me was: 'Lord, do you want me to go to live in Cyprus?' The answer came within the first few days of this five-week-long holiday with God.

But the answer faced me with a bigger, more pressing question. Now that I felt as certain as I could that God was, indeed, calling me to make the island my base, the question was: 'How do I say "Yes" to this request?'

For weeks, I wrote eloquent prayers telling God that I wanted to say 'Yes'. I wrote a poem which brought into sharp focus my fears and longings now that I was confronted with the need to say 'Yes'. I even studied and meditated on the Incarnation of Jesus in the hope that I would gain courage and inspiration from the example of the ready, generous, all-embracing 'Yes' which Mary uttered when the angel invited her to become the mother of the Messiah. Yet, although a burning desire to capitulate consumed me, no 'Yes' so much as squeezed through my lips.

It was on this retreat that I meditated on the word 'grace' which I mentioned in Chapter Five – the grace which is variously translated 'mercy', 'kindness' and 'pure gift'. It was on this retreat that I fell asleep begging for a generous slice of this free gift. It was in the middle of the last night of this retreat, at three in the morning to be precise, that I woke with a joyful, spontaneous 'yes' rising from somewhere deep inside me. It was then that I realised that though we may have earned a degree in theology and have many years of Christian ministry to our credit, left to our own devices, self would still prevent us from saying 'yes' to the freshness and newness of God's unexpected call. Grace is the midwife which gives birth to the desire and the ability to say the 'Yes' which is gestating and growing within us.

Some obstacles to overcome

As I look back on that retreat and as I read the pages of the prayer journal in which I was writing at the time, I notice that a word I used frequently was 'fear'. I was afraid of leaving the English home I loved for a much smaller house in a country where I would always be a foreigner who carried on her person an identity card marked '*ALIEN*'. I was afraid that, at a time when the world seemed gripped by recession, the financial support we would need would not be forthcoming. And I was afraid that, if I were stripped of all the support structures which I had taken for granted for years – the team who worked with me, my spiritual director and others who were there 'for me' whenever I needed them, the quiet places to which I could retreat when I needed a place 'just to be' with God – I would find myself unable to cope.

Others facing the enormity of the 'Yes' which confronts them have spoken to me of similar fears. They are not only natural, they are a gift because they reveal to us that, though we may have been claiming to find our security in God, we have, in fact, been seeking our security in our homes and our salary, our roles and our successes. As Jean Vanier puts it:

> We get seduced by riches and power;
>   by status and by superficial pleasures.
> We begin to doubt
>   and thus tend to float along with the current.[2]

Or, as Ronald Rolheiser points out, as human beings who are creatures of our culture, we spontaneously draw support from fame, hedonism, pleasure, power, possessions, sex and so on. When we are faced with counting the cost of the 'Yes' God wants us to whisper, we are brought face to face with our need to draw strength instead from the resources of God, through the 'littleness' of dependence on him and on his people.

This diagram reminds me of an insight of Jean Vanier's which never ceases to challenge me: 'We all have to choose between two ways of being crazy: the foolishness of the Gospel and the nonsense of the values of the world.'[3]

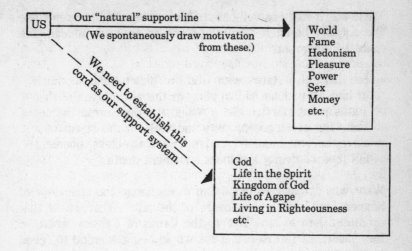

US

Our "natural" support line

(We spontaneously draw motivation from these.)

World
Fame
Hedonism
Pleasure
Power
Sex
Money
etc.

We need to establish this cord as our support system.

God
Life in the Spirit
Kingdom of God
Life of Agape
Living in Righteousness
etc.

Reproduced from Ronald Rotheiser's *The Restless Heart* (Hodder)

The dynamic of love

Those who most easily choose the foolishness of the Gospel are those who are most aware that God is in love with them, that prayer is a love affair with their Creator. The reason for this is that, when we are overtaken by the awareness that we are loved, we are humbled. In particular, we are humbled when the love of *God* overwhelms us. As the Jesuit, John English, observes: 'The intensity of the experience of love is, of course, a great grace. It cannot be obtained by human effort.'[4]

This gift of grace brings in its wake the realisation that we are utterly dependent on Love for our very existence. This realisation opens our eyes to the amazing truth that we are loved, not for anything we can do, but for who we are. We are therefore beings of love – loved even while we were steeped in our sinfulness. This awareness, in turn, draws from us awe, adoration, freedom and a deep desire to serve.

We see this dynamic of love operating so beautifully in Jesus.

What was it that enabled him, of his own free will, to renounce the equality he shared with God and to assume, instead, the guise of a servant?

> He had equal status with God but didn't think so much of himself that he had to cling to the advantages of that status no matter what . . . When the time came, he set aside the privileges of deity and took on the status of a slave, became human! . . . [and] lived a selfless, obedient life [before dying] a selfless, obedient death.[5]

What was it that persuaded him to exchange the splendour of heaven for the rough exposure of the crib? What was it that prompted him to say 'Yes' to the Cross of Calvary when, in the Garden of Gethsemane, his whole being seemed to recoil from the price he had to pay for our salvation?

It was love. Love for the Father. Love for us. In the vocabulary of Jesus, love and service seem to be synonymous. What the Father asked, he did. He could do it because he was motivated by a deep, sustained and sustaining love. As he summed it up on the night before he died: 'I have obeyed my Father's commands and remain in his love' (John 15:10).

When we, too, immerse ourselves in the felt love of God, we will find ourselves wanting to serve. Compelled to serve, not by a Sergeant Major God who barks his commands until we obey, but compelled by love. For the essence of love is service. Lovers delight to find little ways of serving one another – simply to bring delight to the other. Christian service is like that. It is a grateful abandonment and dedication of all that we know of ourselves to all that we know of God. It is as simple, as profound and as costly as that. It is why Paul could call himself, with obvious pride, 'the servant of Christ' (Romans 1:1; Philippians 1:1). It is why Jesus 'consented to be a slave' (Philppians 2:8, JBP); why he could claim: 'The Son of Man did not come to be served, but to serve' (Mark 10:45).

It is why, paradoxically, when we can take for ourselves a life principle which asserts our servanthood, like the caterpillar entering the chrysalis, we find ourselves on the verge of true freedom. Like voluntary slaves who have renounced all personal rights to ownership of possessions, decision-making and self-aggrandisement, and like voluntary slaves who have vowed to spend and be spent in the service of the master they love, we, too, can be slaves, yet gloriously and wonderfully free. This is the foolishness of the Gospel.

How to Serve

There are as many ways of serving God as there are people, and it is vital that we recognise that the first and most important way is simply to be the person he intended us to be.

As someone has summed up this liberating truth: 'A tree brings most glory to God simply by being a tree.'

Yet, so often, as human beings, we strive to become what we are not and consequently grow discouraged and disillusioned in the attempt. We therefore do well to heed another pithy piece of advice: 'Bloom where you are planted.'

A medical student called Vicki helped me to see how profound these simple statements are when I was a patient in the hospital where she was working. I was facing major surgery for the first time in my life. When feelings of apprehension surfaced in me or when fear gripped me, somehow Vicki was always there: to listen, to pray or simply to hold my hand. When I was wheeled into the operating theatre, Vicki was there – grinning broadly with a grin I could interpret as 'I'm praying. I care.' When I came round from the anaesthetic, Vicki was there – still wearing her white coat, still smiling, her china-blue eyes saying: 'I'm glad you survived. I'm still here "for" you.' In the days that followed, she sacrificed much-needed time off to be with me. Her presence was a ministry to me and a witness to the ward. Fellow patients would ask me, 'Who is that young doctor with the beautiful smile?'

And I would tell them: 'She's a member of our church.'

'Church!'

The mention of that word opened up several opportunities for me to speak of God's love and, in particular, to draw alongside a Roman Catholic patient whose need for support and prayer was urgent – all because Vicki was blooming where she was planted, becoming the good doctor God created her to be.

Or I think of another friend who serves God simply by being the person God created her to be. People who meet her often comment: 'I don't know what it is about you, but it's good to be with you.' I felt this even before she became a close friend because, when she prays, it is as though she is really making contact with God. When people speak, she reverences the things they say; when she responds, she is caring and wise; and she seems to find it so easy to affirm others, helping even strangers to feel at home and at peace. She will never wear a recognisable label like 'doctor' or 'politician', but that matters little. She, too, is blooming where she is planted, becoming the beautiful, praying, caring person God created her to be.

In *Call to Conversion*, Jim Wallis underlines the importance of incarnating the love of Christ in this way:

> When I was a university student, I was unsuccessfully evangelised by almost every Christian group on campus. My basic response to their preaching was, 'How can I believe when I look at the way the church lives?' They answered, 'Don't look at the church – look at Jesus.' I now believe that statement is one of the saddest in the history of the church. It puts Jesus on a pedestal apart from the people who name his name. Belief in him becomes an abstraction removed from any demonstration of its meaning to the world. Such thinking is a denial of what is most basic to the gospel: incarnation. People should be able to look at the way we live and begin to understand what the gospel is about. Our life must tell them who Jesus is and what he cares about.[6]

Serving the poor

The briefest of glances at the Gospels reveals that, when Jesus walked this earth, there was a particular group of people he cared about: the poor. As Jean Vanier, himself a champion of the poor, puts it:

It is as though he is attracted in a special way,
almost like a magnet,
to those who are suffering, or broken or rejected.'[7]

It follows that when we find ourselves being drawn closer and closer to Jesus, we shall also find ourselves becoming more and more concerned for the poor. To be with Jesus is to be in the presence of Love and compassion. This compassion is contagious. It will rub off on us and overflow from us, and we will find ourselves asking: 'Who, for me, are the poor?'

I once asked a friend and mentor that question. His answer surprised and challenged me: 'Don't we discover the answer to that question by asking, "How am I poor?"'

The question intrigued and challenged me and, like many such questions, helped me to move forward. I was standing at one of life's cross-roads at the time, sensing that the finger of God was beckoning me to become involved with the poor in some way. When I asked myself the question: 'How am I poor?' the answer rose from somewhere within me:

'My poverty, so often, is a poverty of spirit. I write about prayer as relationship with God and attempt, on retreats and Quiet Days, to lead others to the Fountain of Life, Jesus, but sometimes I do it from the barrenness which can be born of busyness so I feel as though I am scraping the bottom of an empty barrel.'

It was a humbling moment and an important one. Other Christians in leadership, I know full well, suffer from the same dis-ease – particularly Christians who live and work overseas where the resources that people in the West take for granted are so few and far between. As I faced my own poverty, I also found the answer to my question: 'Who, for me, are the poor?'

I not only found the answer to my question, I discovered the nature of my new vocation. I now work full-time with my 'poor' – those who have given everything they have and are for the extension of Christ's Kingdom overseas. Together with my husband, I now have the privilege of leading prayer retreats for them where we seek to take them by the hand, as it were, and stay alongside them in love as they feast on food no money can buy – the banquet of God's love.

While writing this chapter, we have been leading one such retreat and here I have seen the spiritual principle I am spelling out – the interplay between closeness with Christ and compassion for others – transform the perception of a young man in whom God's Spirit is clearly at work. He is someone whose desire to spend quality time with God is deep. While I have been giving him a retreat 'in the stream of life', he has needed to renew his visa so that he can remain in the country where he works. So, together with the refugees who have swarmed into the country where he lives, he joined the long queue of those seeking permission to stay. This gave him ample time to gaze into the lined, helpless, hopeless faces of foreigners far away from home, who, like him, were still struggling to cope with filling in forms in a foreign language. His heart went out to these people in love and in prayer and in the desire to strengthen them in whatever way he could. But, as often happens in such circumstances, this growing desire to help the poor brought him face to face with his own helplessness. As he expressed it to me: 'The task is so enormous. Where do I begin?'

The service of hiddenness

We begin where Jesus began at his birth – by entering into the seeming hopelessness of the situation. Until, like him, we feel to the full the despair and the helplessness, we have not fully identified with the thousands for whom there is no hope of anything but poverty. In two thirds of the world, people are pawns in a political game. They no longer hold the reins of their own lives. The controls were snatched from them or from their forebears decades ago and, like little sticks being swept along by the current of a swollen, fast-flowing river, they simply survive the best they can. Many face abject poverty, starvation, day-in, day-out grief as they watch children and loved-ones young and old die in their arms or, worse, helplessly in the streets. Such destitution may draw the worst rather than the best from them. They may resort to theft, violence or greed but they need the help, the support and the prayers of those God sends across their path – in a queue for a visa, through the medium of the television screen, in the streets of the city where they live.

But where do we begin to make an impact on such a sea of need? The key to that question lies in Matthew 25 where Jesus describes what will happen when he returns, not as a tiny baby but 'in glory'. All the nations will be gathered before him and, just as a Middle Eastern shepherd separates his sheep from his sleek goats, Jesus will call his 'sheep' to him. 'Come!' he will say to them, and he will commend and applaud them for championing the stranger and the starving, the sick and the destitute and those in prison. Whereupon the 'sheep' will express their surprise: 'Lord, when did we see you hungry and feed you, or thirsty and give you something to drink?' And Jesus will reply: 'I tell you the truth, whatever you did for one of the the the least of these brothers of mine, you did for me' (Matthew 25:37, 40).

We may have the time, the energy and the resources to minister to only one of the world's needy ones. It is enough. It may be all that is required of us. Or it may be that our involvement with a sick and suffering world may be through the ministry of hiddenness – either in our own home country or overseas. In *City of Joy*, Dominique Lappierre highlights the value of hiddenness by showing how some of the world's unsung heroes felt called by God to leave home and go to live in one of the worst of India's slums – not to preach, not to engage in overt evangelism, but simply to be a praying presence which incarnated the love of Christ. It was no easy task but it bore fruit for Christ and his Kingdom. Over the long, testing months and years, one young man, in particular, established his rhythm of prayer and involvement with his neighbours, and inspired the kind of trust from which the mutuality of love is born. The impact he made on this forgotten corner of the world can never be fully assessed.

It has been my privilege to visit many such hidden ones –
people who could be climbing the professional ladder in their
home country, people who could be lining their pockets with
the world's gold, but who have chosen, instead, to live and
work quietly in parts of the world where the only thing they
can do for Christ is to incarnate his love and to pray.

Intercessory prayer

The only thing they can do? Yes. Sometimes, such people
see little apparent fruit for their love and their labour. In the
countries where they work, they do not enjoy the kudos of
seeing thousands flock to meetings they speak at. Indeed, there
are no meetings – just a day-in, day-out rhythm of prayer and
overflowing love. Often they feel spiritually drained and dry.
Sometimes they wonder how effective they are. Sometimes
the only sign that God is working through them is that, when
they pray, they weep and they groan as they confront the
darkness in which their part of the world is enveloped. Rather,
I should say, the Holy Spirit weeps through them in the way
Paul describes:

'The Spirit helps us in our weakness. We do not know
what we ought to pray for, but the Spirit himself intercedes
for us with groans that words cannot express. . . . [and] in
accordance with God's will' (Romans 8:26–7).

They groan with the Spirit because the going seems so
hard, because people's hearts seem so hard and the sense of
oppression hangs over them like a thick and menacing cloud.
And yet they stay and they pray and they work and they love
just as Jesus before them stayed and prayed and worked and
loved. The fruit of their labours may not be reaped for decades.
That does not invalidate, rather it authenticates, the power of
the praying presence.

History highlights this. I think, for example, of a letter I
received recently from a friend who spent many years as
a missionary doctor in a little-evangelised country before
returning to his home-land. Some fifteen years later, he was

invited to return to lead seminars in the country where he had once served. It proved to be a moving experience as he discovered that people who were young in years and young in the faith when he had worked with them, had now assumed leadership of the indigenous church. The little fruit he had seen during his time overseas had multiplied one-hundred-fold.

But, of course, we need only to pack our bags and travel overseas if we hear a clear call from God to do so. It is equally possible to work in this hidden way in our own home country. Those of us who do work overseas often testify to sensing the power of the prayer of our supporters, some of whom intercede for us spasmodically, some regularly – like the friends who have our engagement diary tucked into their Bibles or on their notice-board. When some of them write to tell us of the times and ways in which the Holy Spirit has prayed through them or inspired them to pray, the timeliness and aptness of these letters trigger within me tears of gratitude – to God for his faithfulness in raising up such prayer partners and to them for their openness to the Spirit.

The use of our gifts

'But how do I know where I am meant to be serving and what I am supposed to be doing?'

This is a question I am frequently asked. One way of discovering the answer to it is to try to discern the gifts God has entrusted us with.

I make this claim because, as I explained in an earlier chapter, it is the Holy Spirit who, at our creation, and in our re-creation, pours into us the gifts and the talents which are the tools we need for the task to which he calls us. In that chapter, I referred to the way he had equipped Bezalel for the uniqueness of his ministry:

Then the LORD said to Moses, 'See I have chosen Bezalel . . . and I have filled him with the Spirit of God, with skill, ability, and knowledge in all kinds of crafts – to make

artistic designs for work in gold, silver and bronze, to
cut and set stones, to work in wood, and to engage in
all kinds of craftsmanship.

(Exodus 31: 1–5)

God continues:

I have given skill to all the craftsmen to make everything
I have commanded you: the Tent of Meeting, the ark of
the Testimony with the atonement cover on it, and all the
other furnishings of the tent – the table and its articles,
the pure gold lampstand and all its accessories, the altar
of incense, the altar of burnt offering and all its utensils,
the basin with its stand – and also the woven garments,
both the sacred garments for Aaron the priest and the
garments for his sons when they serve as priests, and the
anointing oil and fragrant incense for the Holy Place.

(Exodus 31: 6–11)

I find myself moved by this hive-of-activity picture of a group
of God-gifted people all donating their talents to the glory of
God. I am moved, too, to recall the way in which men and
women of God down the ages have responded to the call to
donate their giftedness to the glory of God.

The day before I began this chapter, for example, I
visited a friend who was listening to Handel's *Messiah*.
How impoverished millions of people would have been if
Handel had failed to translate into that memorable oratorio
the clear prompting of God's Spirit. I think of the short time
I spent in the prayer-saturated studio of an artist in Auckland
on one occasion. I had never met this artist before, though
God had spoken to me through her art. In *Finding God in
the Fast Lane*,[8] I have related how I felt drawn to one of
her paintings which is reproduced in that book. The impact
of that visit continues to bear fruit in my life, bringing me
seemingly endless insights and healing. But we do not need
to be a musician or an artist, an author or a pastor to be
used by God. Some of us have been entrusted with the gift

of hospitality, others with the gift of listening, yet others with a gift of letter writing which God uses to strengthen and comfort the recipients.

When God uses the gifts which he has entrusted us with and gives us glimpses of the ways in which he is using us, we enter into the joy of partnership with our Creator and we take a few further steps along the road to freedom. But God has not only given us gifts; he has created us in rather the same way as he creates children – full of potential. The challenge comes to us at various stages of our lives therefore, to respond to invitations for which we have no experience and for which we do not feel particularly gifted or qualified. When such challenges come from God, we shall find that, latent within us, though we had never discerned them, lie the talents we need for such tasks.

Many Christians would testify that one of the treasures which have come out of the darkness and grimness of the world-wide recession of the 1990s has been the discovery by skilled, professional people that they have gifts which had previously been overlaid by busyness and seeming success. I think of a former director of a company in England.

This businessman, like countless others, was made redundant by the firm he had served faithfully for many years. As he listened to the medley of emotions which vied for his attention – feelings of anger and humiliation, disappointment and loss, he also began to ask God what he was to do with the rest of his life. There seemed little hope that he would be offered secular employment. But did that matter? The question startled him and jolted him out of despondency and into creative thinking. He examined his real situation and realised that although for years he had enjoyed a handsome salary and the high standard of living which went with it, these were not essentials. They were, in fact, luxuries. If he and his family could lower their standard of living, they would have quite enough money to live on.

His family agreed to make the necessary sacrifices and everything changed. As he held on an open palm his perceived need to find new employment, a whole new area of ministry opened up for him. He now finds that he has the time with

God which formerly eluded him and that, from that still place, God is frequently sending him into Eastern Europe to touch the lives of needy believers who so thirst for the ministry of encouragement which he and his wife bring. If my perception is accurate, this family are poorer financially but richer spiritually than they have ever been. They would also be among those who would testify to enjoying more of this mysterious thing called freedom than ever before, because they are allowing God to draw out their full and fine potential.

For personal reflection

1. Make a list of your gifts and abilities. If you find it difficult to do this on your own, ask someone who knows you well to help you. When you have become aware of the way in which God has endowed you, if you feel you can, surrender afresh to him all that you have and all that you are.
2. If you can, pray this prayer

> Take, Lord,
> and receive all my liberty,
> my memory, my understanding
> and my entire will,
> all that I have and possess.
>
> You have given all to me,
> to you, Lord, I return it.
>
> All is yours:
> do with it what you will.
> Give me only your love
> and your grace,
> that is enough for me.[9]

3. Write down your life's motto.
4. Reflect on the following:
   'To love is not to give of your riches but to reveal to others their riches, their gifts, their value and to trust them and their capacity to grow.'[10]

Notes for Chapter Ten

1. Gerard Hughes SJ, *God of Surprises* (Darton, Longman and Todd, 1986) p. 63.
2. Jean Vanier, *The Broken Body* (Darton, Longman and Todd, 1988) p. 118.
3. Jean Vanier, source not traced.
4. John English SJ, *Spiritual Freedom* (Loyola House, 1987), p. 44
5. Philippians 2:6, Eugene Peterson, *The Message* (NavPress, 1993) p. 11
6. Jim Wallis, *Call to Conversion* (Lion, 1981) p. 108.
7. Jean Vanier, *The Broken Body*, p. 13.
8. Joyce Huggett, *Finding God in the Fast Lane* (Eagle, 1993).
9. *The Spiritual Exercises of St Ignatius of Loyola*.
10. Jean Vanier, *The Broken Body*, p. 80.

11

SET FREE BY DIFFICULTIES

I do not want to imply that those who dedicate their lives to the service of God live happily ever after in this world as well as in the next. That would be a travesty of the truth. There is a price to pay for the freedom we seek.

This was brought home to me a few minutes before starting this chapter when I had lunch with a missionary whose husband had died recently and tragically of a heart attack. In the aftermath of his death, his widow and many of his friends found themselves asking that question which has no answer this side of eternity: 'Why?' 'Why, when his ministry was bearing so much fruit, was he taken? Why now?'

While I write, I find myself pausing frequently to pray for two of our own prayer partners whose lives are in turmoil because of the sudden onslaught of life-threatening illness. Having benefited so much from the ministry of this couple, I, too, was tempted to ask the question: 'Why?' But I know from past experience that that question has no answer. Instead, I asked God how I should pray.

As though in answer to that prayer, in the wakeful hours of one night, I was reminded of a silversmith I once watched while I was on holiday in Greece. I had been browsing in his shop for several minutes, admiring his hand-made filigree work and fingering the goblets, chalices and rose bowls he had made when, out of the corner of my eye, I saw him take a pair of tongs and lift a chalice from the shelf in his work corner. Intrigued, I moved to the nearby furnace and watched as he held the chalice in the flames. One part of me wanted to protest. In my *naïveté*, I thought that the gleaming chalice would be spoiled. But

patiently and calmly, he held it in the intensity of the heat.
Then, when his experienced eye detected that the chalice had
been held in the furnace long enough, he withdrew it. Smiling, he
took a soft cloth with which he rubbed his blackened masterpiece
and even I could see that the refining had made his creation even
more beautiful and even more precious than it had been before
its ordeal.

This memory reminded me of a chorus which it is fashionable
to sing in certain Christian circles:

Purify my heart, let me be as gold and precious silver,
Purify my heart, let me be as gold, pure gold.
Refiner's fire, my heart's one desire is to be holy,
set apart for You, Lord . . .

Such powerful, profound and far-reaching words! But if we think
about them and sing them with integrity, perhaps we should not
be surprised when God holds us or those we love and admire
in the flames? If we believe those words, we shall know, with a
deep-down certainty, that he will hold us there just long enough
for the refining to take place but he will never abandon us to the
flames. As someone has put it: 'He who is near me is near the
fire.' Even so, being purified in this way will inevitably hurt. It
is part of the price we pray for our freedom.

The pruning principle

We must remember, too, that when Jesus likened himself to the
whole vine and likened us to individual branches, he warned us
that his Father is a faithful vine-dresser. Faithful vine-dressers
always prune the branches that have borne fruit so that they
can bear more fruit. When I watch the vine-dressers near my
home lopping off branch after branch from their vines, leaving
little more than a leprous stump, I sometimes wonder how the
vine might feel if it were sentient. Would it protest: 'Why this
cruelty? Why this waste?' Or would it look back on past prunings

and recognise that the cutting back is, indeed, an essential part of the fruit-bearing process?

We have no way of telling how a vine might feel. Many of us, however, have felt the pain of loss as the heavenly vine-dresser has lopped off the muchness and manyness of our ministries and brought us to the place where we are prepared to do the one thing he asks and to do it with all the wisdom and energy he gives. We have recognised that this is part of the price we pay for our freedom. We have also discovered the paradox that, when we submit to such drastic pruning, we find ourselves feeling not empty but full, not restricted or deprived but enriched and liberated. We find ourselves free to blossom in the place where he wants us to be. Free to bear fruit in the manner in which he always intended. Free to become the people he always created us to be.

Spiritual warfare

But there is another reason why the price of freedom is high. As Peter warns us, we have an Arch-enemy to contend with. This enemy 'prowls around like a roaring lion looking for someone to devour' (1 Peter 5:8). Although he does not seem to trouble Christians whose lives resemble the Sadducees Jesus once confronted with the condemnation: 'You do not know the Scriptures or the power of God' (Matthew 22:29), he does torment believers who perceive Jesus to be the pearl of great price for whom it is worth sacrificing everything. Such Christians often find themselves paying a very high price for the freedom to become the people God created them to be. They know what Michael Green means when he warns that, when we surrender our lives to Christ, 'we pass from security into the firing line'.[1] They understand, too, John's description of the enemy in the Book of Revelation where he is likened to a blood-thirsty dragon which wages constant war against those who keep God's commandments and bear testimony to Jesus (Revelation 12).

Because the enemy's wiles are so subtle and so potentially

lethal, it can be helpful to highlight them so that when he does his worst, we recognise what is happening and recognise who holds the reins and what is really happening to us.

The accuser

One way of clarifying the mystery is to become conversant with the enemy's many names. These indicate his many activities. One name is Satan and, as Michael Green reminds us in *I Believe in Satan's Downfall*, the word 'Satan' means 'accuser' or 'slanderer'. We may expect, therefore, to suffer the indignity of being accused before God by Satan and others who insist that we are unacceptable. In Zechariah 3:1, we see the high priest Joshua being assailed in this way:

'Then the Angel showed me (in my vision) Joshua the High Priest standing before the Angel of the Lord; and Satan was there too, at the Angel's right hand, accusing Joshua of many things' (LB).

We see Satan playing a similar trick in Job 1:6–14 (LB):

One day as the angels came to present themselves before the Lord. Satan, the Accuser, came with them.

'Where have you come from?' the Lord asked Satan.

And Satan replied, 'From patroling the earth.'

Then the Lord asked Satan, 'Have you noticed my servant Job? He is the finest man in all the earth – a good man who fears God and will have nothing to do with evil.'

'Why shouldn't he, when you pay him so well?' Satan scoffed. 'You have always protected him and his home and his property from all harm. You have prospered everything he does – look how rich he is! No wonder he "worships" you! But just take away his wealth, and you'll see him curse you to your face!' . . .

So Satan went away; and sure enough, not long afterwards when Job's sons and daughters were dining at the oldest brother's house, tragedy struck.

And just as we read of Satan entering into Judas during the Last

Supper (Luke 22:3), so Satan seems to have entered into Job's wife and 'Job's comforters' as his so-called friends are often described. Through them, Satan accuses Job before God and the result is that Job is filled with self-loathing, self-condemnation and the desire to die:

'Oh, that God would grant the thing I long for most – to die beneath his hand, and be freed from his painful grip' (Job 6:8–9, LB).

The pattern spelled out so painstakingly in the Book of Job has been repeated countless times down the centuries so that Christian is set against Christian. Where love, compassion and tenderness should abound, hatred, bitterness and a critical spirit reign. Instead of learning to understand each other and rejoicing in the insights which God has entrusted to others, so-called followers of Jesus revile each other, become entrenched in the narrowness of their cherished beliefs, and fight tooth and nail to defend the little portion of the truth which they believe to be the whole truth.

Though most would not stoop to actual murder, they crucify others with hatred in their eyes, and vehemence, cruelty and bigotry in their verbal attacks. And Satan chuckles because, as anyone with a grain of sensitivity knows, the adage, 'sticks and stones may break my bones but words will never hurt me' is far from the truth. Words do hurt. They inflict deep and lasting wounds which may take years to heal.

Worse, Satan rubs his hands with glee because, while Jesus continues to pray 'that they may be one' (John 17:11), the Accuser has kept on the boil the scandal of the disunity, distrust and discord which has riddled the church for centuries, marring the image of Christ it presents to a world which is rightly scandalised by this perennial denial of the power of the Gospel.

The tempter

Satan is also known as the Tempter (Matthew 4:3; 1 Thessalonians 3:5). Just as the Tempter sidled alongside Adam and Eve in Genesis 3 and alongside Jesus in the Wilderness, so he will frequently sidle alongside us, seeking to alienate us from God. For Satan is the Antichrist,

> the embodiment of opposition to our Lord . . . He is set for our downfall, and will come at us either as the king of the jungle, the 'roaring lion seeking whom he may devour' (1 Peter 5:8) or else seductively, as the 'angel of light' (2 Corinthians 11:14) seeking whom he may deceive.[2]

He is not only the tempter *par excellence*, he is a liar. Jesus goes so far as to call him 'the father of lies' (John 8:44). We hear him whispering lies into the ears of Adam and Eve in the Garden of Eden and, similarly, we shall hear him whispering lies into our minds and hearts, causing us to doubt God's love and promises.

Sadly, that is not all. This subtle liar and tempter does not work alone. He is the prince of the power of the air who has hosts of evil spirits on whose help he draws. As Paul describes this network of evil:

> We are not fighting against people made of flesh and blood, but against persons without bodies – the evil rulers of the unseen world, those mighty satanic beings and great evil princes of darkness who rule this world; and against huge numbers of wicked spirits in the spirit world.
>
> (Ephesians 6:12, LB)

The novels of Frank Peretti have opened our eyes and imaginations to the reality of that claim as it might well be fleshed out in our materialistic, Western, secular society, so that it is now easy to see how leaders in all walks of life, including the church, have been influenced by this enemy Jesus calls 'the prince of this world' (John 12:31; 14:30).

As Richard Foster perceives the situation:

> Behind absentee landlords of ghetto flats are the spiritual forces of greed and avarice. Behind unreasoned and excessive resistance to the Gospel message are

demonic forces of disobedience and distraction. Underneath the organized structures of injustice and oppression are principalities of privilege and status. Aiding and abetting the sexual violence and the race hate and the child molestation that are such a part of modern society are diabolical powers of destruction and brutality. Therefore, says Paul, when we face, for instance, people who are deaf to the Gospel or laws that are cruel and unjust or leaders who are oppressive, then we are also dealing with cosmic principalites and powers that are straight from the pit.[3]

Or, as Michael Green sums up the situation:

Satan attacks the minds of men with doubts, fears and propaganda. Satan assails the spirits of men with lust, pride and hatred. Satan assaults the bodies of men with disease, torture and death. Satan assails the institutions of men (which he seeks to impregnate) with structural evil. In the Bible itself we find him manipulating nations (Daniel 10), city councils (1 Thessalonians 2:18), rioting mobs (John 8:44, 59) and the very elements themselves (Mark 4:39). Satan is immensely powerful. It is unwise to underestimate him.[4]

The oppressor

In particular, it is unwise to underestimate his ability to oppress us and, through constant discouragement, over-work, criticism or sickness, to grind us into the ground like powder until we reach the conclusion that only one option faces us – to give up.

Just as we have observed him doing just this to Job, so we watch him achieve the same aim with the prophet Elijah. Having won an immense prayer victory for God on Mount Carmel, the exhausted Elijah falls prey to the twin curses of a distorted perception of his person and ministry, and the discouragement which led to depression and a gnawing, numbing death wish. So we hear this great prayer warrior bleating before God:

'I have had enough, Lord . . . Take my life' (1 Kings 19:4).

The first part of that pain-wracked prayer is being echoed today by countless Christians seeking to become the people God created them to be. I have met them in England – fine, dedicated people, including Christians in leadership, who sacrifice so much for God. In particular, since I have had the privilege of working overseas, I have met such people in countries where the going is tough because the blanket of spiritual darkness never seems to lift; where the signs of the movement of the Spirit in people's lives are so few and far between that they wonder why they are there, question whether they should pack their bags and return home, or ask soul-searching questions like: 'What are we doing wrong?' or 'Why can't we make more impact for God?' And I have encountered such spiritual oppression myself.

Just before writing this chapter, for example, my husband and I were speaking at a conference where the hardness of hearts of some of the so-called believers crushed us so effectively that I felt powerless to speak or to minister in the way I had planned. Like Elijah, I, too, wanted to escape – to run away, to lick my wounds, to give up. I resisted that temptation and faced, instead, the heartbreak of watching Jesus's parable of the sower being enacted before my eyes: God's precious seed falling on calloused hearts; some being swept away in the foaming sea of frivolity and the desire some Christians have to be entertained rather than taught; other seed being choked by cynicism and the pull of the peer group. Although there *was* the joy, too, of watching some seed bear beautiful fruit for the Kingdom, I came away with the overwhelming and growing sense that we had been embroiled in enemy activity and that we and the group with whom we had been working had been ill-equipped to combat God's Arch-enemy.

The seducer

But perhaps we need to remember that Satan comes to us most subtly, not through external circumstances or other people, but through our own attitudes, thought patterns, personality, emotions and imagination. As John English emphasises, Satan's aim is to enslave us, to turn us in on ourselves, to make us self-centred, to make obsessions of our own egotisms: 'No single individual of any state in life is overlooked: Satan wages a war that involves the whole universe. His intention is to reduce [people] to slavery and thus prevent them from reaching their completion and fulfilment.'[5]

He seduces us, too, by attacking our Achilles' heel – particularly in those unguarded moments which creep up on us all when we are exhausted or suffering from any kind of stress.

'Is it worth it?' That is the question some Christians ask when they find themselves, like Job and Elijah, being jolted through month after month of turbulence. The answer to that question, if Jesus is to be believed, is a resounding 'Yes'. In the Book of Revelation, he piles promise after promise upon 'the overcomers'. As John describes the triumphant scene:

> I, John, saw the Holy City, the new Jerusalem, coming down from God out of heaven. It was a glorious sight, beautiful as a bride at her wedding.
>
> I heard a loud shout from the throne saying, 'Look, the home of God is now among men, and he will live with them and they will be his people; yes, God himself will be among them. He will wipe away all tears from their eyes, and there shall be no more death, nor sorrow, nor crying, nor pain. All of that has gone forever.'
>
> And the one sitting on the throne said, 'See, I am making all things new!' . . . Everyone who conquers will inherit all these blessings and I will be his God and he will be my son.'
>
> (Revelation 21:2–5,7, LB)

But the good news is that we do not need to wait until the Lord's return to enter into our inheritance. We can enjoy foretaste after foretaste of the promised freedom now. For just as a woodcarver takes a sleeping piece of wood into his hands and with a skilled stroke here and a deft cut there sets the wood free to be the carved bird or figurine it begs to be, so the eye of God sees our potential and makes of life's problems,

and even the murderous wiles of the Evil One, the chisel which
transforms us rather than the axe which destroys us.

Co-operating with God

Think again of Job, for example. Bruised, battered and bleeding
though he was, God granted him graced moments when, clearly,
he was being set free to emerge as the person of faith God
created him to be. Even before God had restored his fortunes,
he could give that immortal testimony:

'I know that my Redeemer lives, and that he will stand upon
the earth at last. And I know that after this body has decayed,
this body shall see God! Then he will be on *my* side! Yes, I
shall see him, not as a stranger, but as a friend! What a glorious
hope!' (Job 19:25–7, LB).

And as he emerged from the crucible, he could make this
jubilant faith statement before God:

'I had heard about you before, but now I have seen you'
(Job 42:5).

God's longing is that each of us should emerge equally
unscathed, humbled, yet triumphant. So he suggests a series of
coping mechanisms for those times when the going is tough.

Peter highlights one:

> Be careful – watch out for attacks from Satan, your great
> enemy. He prowls around like a hungry, roaring lion,
> looking for some victim to tear apart. Stand firm when
> he attacks. Trust the Lord; and remember that other
> Christians all around the world are going through these
> sufferings too.
>
> (1 Peter 5:8–9, LB)

Or, as Richard Foster puts it:

> Spiritual warfare is not something we talk about; it is
> something we do. How do we do it? . . . We do it by
> coming against every 'mountain' that hinders our progress

in God. . . . We stand against evil thoughts and suspicions and distortions of every sort. . . . We do it by demon expulsion. Wherever we find evil forces at work, we firmly demand that they leave. We are in charge, not them. In the ministry of power we take authority over whatever is opposed to our life in the kingdom of God.[6]

When we do stand firm and learn to take authority over our sexual fantasies, worldly attitudes and self-centred thoughts, instead of caving in to every temptation which comes our way, eventually we experience a curious sense of exhilaration, joy and lightness of spirit. Although we may have learned from the bitterness of experience that Ole Hallesby was correct when he claimed that 'the secret prayer chamber is a bloody battle-ground. Here violent and decisive battles are fought out',[7] we now know from experience that, when those battles are won, we find ourselves in touch with the person God always intended us to be. It is a jubilant and triumphant moment.

Striving together

Such moments motivate us to heed other injuctions given by God – like his exhortation to learn to fight the enemy rather than each other. Through his mouth-piece, Paul, God encourages us to arm ourselves for battle, and, like Roman soldiers, to take up our shields and form a solid phalanx of faith which can resist all the fiery darts of the enemy (Ephesians 6:13–16). This way we shall experience that unity of the Spirit with which we can contend those who oppose us 'as one man', not frightened by anything (Philippians 1:27). This way, the truth of James 4:7 becomes experiential rather than theoretical: 'Resist the devil and he will flee from you.'

This resistance includes Satan's activity within the innermost core of our own being. And, if we are to detect his activity accurately, like Elijah, we need times of stillness and reflection so that we can hear God's still small voice:

'Go out and stand before me on the mountain,' the Lord

told [Elijah]. And as Elijah stood there the Lord passed by, and a mighty windstorm hit the mountain; it was such a terrible blast that the rocks were torn loose, but the Lord was not in the wind. After the wind, there was an earthquake, but the Lord was not in the earthquake. And after the earthquake, there was a fire, but the Lord was not in the fire. And after the fire, there was the sound of a gentle whisper. When Elijah heard it, he wrapped his face in his scarf and went out and stood at the entrance of the cave.

And a voice said, 'Why are you here, Elijah?'

(1 Kings 19:11–13, LB)

There is value, I find, in establishing a rhythm of prayer which includes daily times of stillness during which God can gently help us to sense where his Spirit has been at work within us and where the Evil One has been undermining the Holy Spirit's work. This can connect us so powerfully with the person we were created to be that it is well worth the discipline.

One way of embarking on this form of listening to God and one's self is to set aside a few minutes each day when we watch an action replay of the past twenty-four hours. The aim is not to condemn ourselves but simply to be aware of the things we have done and left undone; the things, too, we have thought and the way we have reacted. Often we will see clearly that the Holy Spirit has been very active in our lives, keeping us focused on God and keeping us journeying in a God-ward direction. From time to time, however, as we reflect, we may well become conscious that, though we began the day well, gradually our attitudes and actions became more self-centred than God-centred. On such occasions, we should suspect that the Evil One has been at work and that we have colluded with him. When we detect his devilish dealings there is further value in tracing the thought or attitude or reaction back to its beginning. This way, we shall not only deal a death-blow to this current insurrection, but we shall learn how to detect the deceiver's presence more quickly and, in future, to nip his activities in the bud.

Another way of discerning the intrusion of the Evil One is to listen to the language of our moods. As Ignatius of Loyola pointed out so helpfully, when we are becoming the person God created us to be, entering into the fullness of his freedom, the Holy Spirit's activity in us 'is very delicate, gentle, and often delightful. It may be compared to the way a drop of water penetrates a sponge.'⁸ When Satan 'tries to interrupt our progress, the movement is violent, disturbing, and confusing. It may be compared to the way a waterfall hits a stone ledge below.'⁹

Looking to Jesus

When our reflection reveals the presence of the Evil One, there is no need to despair. As we have already seen, God, not Satan, holds the reins because God and not Satan is in ultimate control. And if we listen carefully, we may hear the kind of heavenly music Joshua heard when he was being accused before God by Satan:

'And the Lord said to Satan, "I reject your accusations, Satan; yes, I, the Lord, . . . rebuke you. I have decreed mercy to Joshua and his nation; they are like a burning stick pulled out of the fire."' (Zechariah 3:2 LB).

Or we may hear God rebuke our accusers as Job heard him rebuke his three friends:

'I am angry with you . . . for you have not been right in what you have said about me, as my servant Job was' (Job 42:7, LB).

For, on the Cross, Jesus conquered evil and the Evil One. By his death, Jesus rescued us from the clutches of all dark, Satanic principalities and powers. That is why Luther's hymns and catechisms 'reverberate with joy that God has rescued us from the "monster" or "tyrant" the devil, who previously held us in the captivity of sin, law, curse and death'. That is why we can echo Paul's cry:

I am convinced that nothing can ever separate us from [God's] love. Death can't, and life can't. The angels won't,

and all the powers of hell itself cannot keep God's love
away. Our fears for today, our worries about tomorrow
. . . nothing will ever be able to separate us from the love
of God demonstrated by our Lord Jesus Christ when he
died for us.

(Romans 8:38–9, LB)

That is why, even when the world and Satan have done their
worst, like Jesus returning to Galilee from the Wilderness of
Temptation, we shall be able to return to our Galilee 'full of
the Holy Spirit's power' (Luke 4:14, LB) – a little more like the
person God always intended us to be.

For personal reflection

1. Watch an action replay of the past twenty-four hours. Try
   not to judge yourself but simply to recall the events and
   your reactions to them. Ask the Holy Spirit to shed his
   light on the memories, showing you where you have been
   responding positively to his promptings and where and how
   Satan has been active in your life: by accusing you before
   God, tempting you, oppressing you, seducing you. . . .
2. While these memories are fresh in your mind, if you recall
   occasions when you have resisted the Evil One, thank God
   for giving you the grace. If you recall occasions when you
   failed to resist temptation, refuse to grovel. Instead, remind
   yourself that we shall regularly fail unless we receive from
   God the grace we need to resist. Receive his forgiveness
   and stride on towards freedom.
3. Re-read the story of the silversmith on pp. 157–8. Do you
   know of anyone who is being 'held in the fire' at the moment?
   If so, hold them in the love of God.
4. Pray, too, for those whose ministries and lives are being
   pruned in any way and especially for those who work in
   countries where the sense of oppression is marked and
   persistent.

Notes for Chapter Eleven

1. Michael Green, *I Believe in Satan's Downfall* (Hodder and Stoughton, 1984) p. 60.
2. Michael Green, *I Believe in Satan's Downfall*, p. 48.
3. Richard Foster, *Prayer* (Hodder and Stoughton, 1992) pp. 254–5.
4. Michael Green, *I Believe in Satan's Downfall*, p. 50.
5. John J. English SJ, *Spiritual Freedom* (Loyola House, Guelph, 1987) p. 164.
6. Richard Foster, *Prayer*, p. 256.
7. Ole Hallesby, quoted by Richard Foster, in *Prayer*, p. 255.
8. *The Spiritual Exercises of St Ignatius*, trans. David L. Fleming SJ (The Institute of Jesuit Resources, 1985) p. 217.
9. *The Spiritual Exercises of St Ignatius*, trans. David L. Fleming SJ, p. 217.
10. John Stott, *The Cross of Christ* (Inter-Varsity Press, 1986) p. 229.

12

FREE AT LAST

Most days when I am at home, I go on an hour-long prayer walk. It takes me past the vineyards which I have described in an earlier chapter, through the orange and lemon groves, along the beach and back through the vineyards again. I did this walk just before starting to type this chapter and I am glad I did because what I saw seemed to sum up much of the content of this book.

As I wandered along those now-scorched vine terraces, I noticed first that tufts of lush, resilient grass had already begun to push their way through the parched earth and past the layer of ashes. Then, when I stooped down on a certain hillock to examine this seeming miracle more closely, I marvelled. At my feet lay a carpet of tiny, blue flowers – like wild grape-hyacinths. These, too, had survived the flames, broken through the rock-hard earth and blossomed in the way their Creator intended. They seemed to smile in the warm, autumn sunshine. They seemed free indeed.

Their simple but stunning beauty reminded me of the freedom we shall all enjoy one day. John's description of it never ceases to enthrall me:

'Dear friends, now we are children of God, and what we will be has not yet been made known. But we know that when he appears, we shall be like him, for we shall see him as he is' (1 John 3:2).

'When he appears.' When Jesus appears again we shall be free at last: free from every vestige of self-centredness, free from sin, free from temptation, free to be with him, free to become the person he always intended us to be. The world may scoff and scorn but it cannot steal our joy as we anticipate that day.

This waiting reminds me of a moving scene in Richard Attenborough's memorable, award-winning film, *Ghandi*. The cameras take us to a remote railway station in India. There we see a platform teeming with waiting Indians. Two British soldiers survey the scene from their hill-top vantage-point. Nodding towards the crowd as a steam train approaches, one asks: 'What are they doing? What are they waiting for?'

His colleague replies: 'I've no idea. All I know is they received a telegram a few days ago. On it were three words: "He is coming".'

The train snorted to a halt. A small, middle-aged Indian dressed in white home-spun cloth alighted. The people surged forward to greet him. Dark eyes lit up, weary faces creased with smiles. And the soldiers mocked at the reverence with which this seemingly insignificant native was being treated. Why the euphoria? Here was just another Indian, here today, gone tomorrow. Gone tomorrow? They were not to know that this charismatic figure, Ghandi, would one day lead his country into freedom from British rule. The thought had never even crossed their minds.

Neither can the world concede that our telegram from heaven has arrived. 'I am coming soon,' Jesus promises (Revelation 3:11). The world cannot detect the joy which wells up within us like a fountain as we read his further promise, 'I am making everything new!' (Revelation 21:5). The world does not understand that when he comes, we shall be transformed into the people he created us to be. We shall be free at last. Yet this is the theme which throbs through the Book of Revelation. Whenever we meditate on the mysteries concealed in the pages of this book, we stand on the threshold of Paradise found. Freedom found.

Has anyone captured the atmosphere more accurately than C.S. Lewis as he concludes his famous Narnia tales? Here he claims that the things which happened to his characters after the books ended were so great and beautiful that he could not write them. Although for us it was the end of all the stories, for them it was the beginning of the real story.

> All their life in this world and all their adventures in Narnia had only been the cover and the title page: now at last they were beginning Chapter One of the Great Story which no one on earth has read: which goes on for ever: in which every chapter is better than the one before.[1]

In the Book of Revelation, too, every chapter is more thrilling than the one before. Reading the book at one sitting is as tantalising as hearing the sound of running water when climbing in the mountains on a hot summer's day, and as thirst-quenching as drinking long draughts from such crystal-clear streams. Each promise is precious: the promise of 'a new heaven and a new earth', the promise that God will 'wipe away every tear from [our] eyes', the promise that 'death shall be no more, and never again shall there be sorrow or crying or pain' (21:1–4). But the greatest thrill of all will be that we shall see the Beloved face to face. He will make our home with us and we with him. We shall be his people and he will be with us. We shall delight, not in his presents, but in his everlasting presence.

Free to worship

And, for the first time in our lives, we shall be set free truly to worship. Some of us have already received a foretaste of what the worship of heaven might entail – complete self-forgetfulness, utter self-abandonment. As John describes it:

> Day and night they never stop saying:
>
>> 'Holy, holy, holy,
>> is the Lord God Almighty,
>> who was and is, and is to come.' . . .
>
> Then I looked and heard the voice of many angels, numbering thousands upon thousands, and ten thousand times

ten thousand. They encircled the throne and the living
creatures and the elders. In a loud voice they sang:

> 'Worthy is the Lamb, who was slain, to receive power
> and wealth and wisdom and strength
> and honour and glory and praise!'

Then I heard every creature in heaven and on earth and
under the earth and on the sea, and all that is in them,
singing:

> 'To him who sits on the throne and to the Lamb
> be praise and honour and glory and power,
> for ever and ever!'

The four living creatures said, 'Amen,' and the elders fell
down and worshipped.

(Revelation 4:8; 5:11–14)

I am tempted to say, 'Fantastic!' and to leave it at that. But
there is more.

Free for Intimacy

Zephaniah puts it beautifully:

'Do not fear . . . do not let your hands hang limp. The LORD
your God is with you, he is mighty to save. He will take great
delight in you, he will quiet you with his love, he will rejoice
over you with singing', (3:16–17).

There is a sense in which that prophecy has already been
fulfilled. There is another sense in which we have yet to enter
into a full experiential awareness of its meaning. Here in this
world, God's felt presence is, at best, fleeting, intermittent,
transitory. Not so in heaven. There we shall enjoy a permanent
intimacy with God. There, we shall know, not with the eye
of faith, but experientially that we belong to God and that he
belongs to us. There the words from the Song of Solomon will
find their fulfilment:

'I am my Beloved's, and my Beloved is mine' (6:3, JB).

We shall know what it means to be the Bride of Christ. Michael Wilcock's description of the heavenly Bride never ceases to excite me:

We have passed beyond the bounds of space and time into regions of eternal light, unshadowed by the slightest imperfection, not to say evil; where the eyes of every created thing are fixed in adoration upon the Lamb alone. *Yet he is not alone.* For sharing the Scene with him – indeed, taking its very title role – is a radiant stranger whose features, as we consider them, are nonetheless familiar. Can it be . . .?

It is 'the Bride, the wife of the Lamb.' It is the church of Christ. *It is you; it is I.* Whatever other metaphors we may use to describe our relationship with Christ, the last Scene of the Bible shows us ourselves married to him, 'cleansed . . . by the washing of water with the word', presented before him 'in splendour, without spot or wrinkle or any such thing' (Ephesians 5:26–7).

Although there we must leave the portals of heaven, we may continue to feast our minds on these mysteries remembering that, while we live life in the overlap, we are rather like butterflies testing our wings in a vast auditorium. We are no longer caterpillars. We have multi-coloured wings already. And we have learned that flying is fun. But, from time to time, we press against the window-pane sensing that a greater freedom is only a pane of glass away. It is. And Christ is coming soon. When he comes, the glass panels will be removed. We shall be free at last. Free to become the people he always created us to be.

Even so, come Lord Jesus!

Notes for Chapter Twelve

1. C.S. Lewis, *The Last Battle* (Puffin, 1964) p. 165.
2. Michael Wilcock, *I Saw Heaven Opened* (Inter-Varsity Press, 1975) p. 205.